The Source® for Autism

by Gail J. Richard, Ph.D.

D1605391

Skill	Ages
■ autism	■ All Ages

Evidence-Based Practice

According to the American Speech-Language-Hearing Association *Guidelines for Speech-Language Pathologists in Diagnosis, Assessment, and Treatment of Autism Spectrum Disorders Across the Life Span, Roles and Responsibilities of Speech-Language Pathologists in Diagnosis, Assessment, and Treatment of Autism Spectrum Disorders Across the Life Span,* and *Knowledge and Skills Needed by Speech-Language Pathologists for Diagnosis, Assessment, and Treatment of Autism Spectrum Disorders Across the Life Span* (ASHA 2006, www.asha.org/members/ deskref-journal/deskref/default), the following principles are supported:

- Speech-language pathologists have responsibilities for engaging in screening, diagnosis, assessment and intervention, working with families, collaboration, professional development, research, and advocacy in regard to autism spectrum disorders.

- Nonverbal and verbal communication behaviors and deficits need to be addressed in treatment goals.

- Enhancing social communication development and the quality of life in individuals with autism spectrum disorders is a critical role for professionals.

- Differential diagnosis of autism subtypes is a significant challenge.

- Social communication deficits can be used to qualify students with Asperger and high-functioning autism for support services.

- Informal observation of characteristic behaviors should supplement formal assessment.

- Functional communication is a priority for programming in autism spectrum disorders.

The information and interventions in this book incorporate these principles and are based on expert professional practice.

LinguiSystems®

LinguiSystems, Inc.
3100 4th Avenue
East Moline, IL 61244
800-776-4332

FAX: 800-577-4555
E-mail: service@linguisystems.com
Web: linguisystems.com

Printed in the U.S.A.
ISBN 10: 0-7606-0146-1
ISBN 13: 978-0-7606-0146-4

About the Author

Gail J. Richard, Ph.D., CCC/SLP is a professor at Eastern Illinois University in the Department of Communication Disorders & Sciences, Charleston, Illinois. Gail's specialty area within speech-language pathology is child/adolescent language disorders, specifically language learning disabilities, language processing disorders, autism, and selective mutism. Prior to joining the faculty at Eastern, she taught in the public schools for four years. Her current responsibilities include teaching graduate and undergraduate classes, as well as supervision in the university clinic. Gail has presented workshops throughout the country and consults with numerous school districts on diagnostic and educational programming issues. In her almost 20 years of experience as a speech-language pathologist, she has seen hundreds of clients with autism and developmental disabilities.

Gail's professional honors and awards include Past President of the Illinois Speech-Language-Hearing Association, Fellow of the Illinois Speech-Language-Hearing Association, member of the Legislative Council of the American Speech-Language-Hearing Association, and four Faculty Excellence Awards at Eastern Illinois University. Gail also serves as the NCAA Faculty Athletics Representative for Eastern Illinois University. Gail's previous publications with LinguiSystems include the *Language Processing Test* and the *Language Processing Kit*, co-authored with Mary Anne Hanner.

Dedication

To all of the individuals with autism whom I had the pleasure of meeting and interacting with over the years, as well as their parents, teachers, families, and friends. You have been my source of inspiration, energy, and commitment. I have learned invaluable lessons in courage, humor, dedication, and creativity. Thank you for touching my life and allowing me to be part of yours.

Table of Contents

Introduction

No two autistic children are alike. What may work successfully for one
will not work for another. It is true there are specific principles of
learning that run through all human endeavors. The goal is to observe
and find the specific pattern of response each child exhibits, then move
from there.

Temple Grandin, Ph.D.
Emergence: Labeled Autistic

Autism is a complex, fascinating, challenging disability! The complexity of
autism contributes to many of the existing misconceptions and myths which
surround the label *autism*. The term itself has been around since the 1940s,
but a clear understanding of the disorder and techniques for modifying its
symptoms continue to confuse and intimidate parents and professionals.

Autism is a syndrome disorder, which means there are several variables or
characteristics that must be present for an accurate diagnosis. The syndrome
aspect is the reason that autism is often illustrated using pieces of a puzzle.
Four distinct diagnostic pieces must be evidenced for autism. However, many
additional characteristics are often part of an individual's autism puzzle. The
characteristics of the autism syndrome can be very severe or very mild. In
addition, the configuration of the various pieces influences how each individual
actually presents the disability. The pieces of the syndrome account for the
challenge in diagnosis and remedial programming.

While there are common pieces in every autism puzzle, the way each puzzle
actually fits together will vary with each individual with the syndrome. The
diagnosis must be accurate in identifying the syndrome of autism, as well as
the individual component pieces. Poorly-defined diagnosis within the syndrome
can result in ineffective intervention.

Many available treatment options offer hope of "cures, miracles," and "normal
life" to parents of children with autism. Professionals and families need to
differentiate the variables in each client's autism syndrome carefully to make

appropriate remediation decisions. If the individual doesn't demonstrate a particular characteristic, then investing in treatment for that characteristic probably won't be beneficial. However, early intervention is a critical factor in prognosis. Families and professionals need assistance in determining the specific needs of an individual with autism so that intervention can begin impacting the disability as soon as possible.

The Source for Autism serves as an eclectic review of autism — its definition, diagnostic characteristics, intervention strategies, and general suggestions for the team of individuals who work to accomplish the highest potential possible within the disability. The focus of this book is clinical, rather than theoretical. It is a hands-on resource for those "in the trenches" every day, trying to make a difference in human lives. The goal is to provide functional information which will instill confidence as you approach the syndrome of autism. That confidence may result in an appreciation for the incredible, exciting challenge autism presents!

Gail

Chapter 1
Definition of Autism

Autism is a developmental disorder. A defect in the systems
which process incoming sensory information causes the child to
overreact to some stimuli and underreact to others. The autistic
child often withdraws from her environment and the people in it
to block out an onslaught of incoming stimuli.

Temple Grandin
Emergence: Labeled Autistic

Myths about Autism

The first published accounts of autism were by Dr. Leo Kanner in 1943.
Dr. Kanner described a population of individuals who were very isolated
and aloof — hence the term *autism*. Autism means "self," and the group
Kanner studied appeared to be locked in an internally-focused world.
Additional characteristics noted by Dr. Kanner included communication
deficits, an insistence on sameness, motor differences, and onset during
the first few years of life. Research has refined definitions of the disorder through the years, yet the main features identified by Kanner
have remained surprisingly constant.

The aspect that has not remained constant is an understanding of cause,
prognosis, and remediation within the autistic spectrum. Numerous
myths and misconceptions about autism continue to exist today across
professionals. Dated literature in the area of autism substantiates
inaccurate perceptions that are passed on in error.

One example is the myth of "refrigerator parents." At one time, a study
of parents of children with autism demonstrated that the parents, particularly mothers, were non-emotional and subdued with their children.
This study resulted in the erroneous cause-effect assumption that the
non-affectionate parent had caused the child's internal emotional shutdown. We now understand that the parents' reactions were modified
in response to their child's disability, not the other way around. Yet I
continue to be amazed by how many parents have been told that, in
some way, they caused or are responsible for their child's disability!

Before defining the disability, it is important to erase some of the misper-
ceptions that persist regarding autism — to strip away old untruths.
Jean Madsen Beisler, a speech-language pathologist at the University
of Iowa Child Psychiatric Clinic, often used a list of myths at the beginning of her talks to address "wrong" ideas before introducing correct

information. The list has been modified some here, but it serves a similar purpose. It's a simple true/false test, so you have a 50% chance of being correct, even if you guess. Good luck!

Autism Myths & Misunderstandings

1. Children with autism do not make progress.

2. Children with autism do not smile at you.

3. Children with autism are not affectionate.

4. Autism can be outgrown.

5. Children with autism are retarded.

6. Children with autism do not make eye contact.

7. Children with autism do not relate to peers and adults.

8. Children with autism cannot be tested by conventional means.

9. Children with autism demonstrate behaviors that cannot be changed.

10. Maladaptive behaviors must be extinguished before remediation can begin.

11. Children with autism do not notice people or things in the environment.

12. Underneath the autism is a normal child, if you can discover the key.

---

1. Children with autism do not make progress.

False. Children with autism make a great deal of progress, especially when intervention begins during the preschool years. There are some variables that can restrict the scope of progress, but almost without exception, remarkable progress is possible. For this reason, parents and professionals must strive to remain current in intervention techniques so they can facilitate improvement throughout the child's life.

2. Children with autism do not smile at you.

False. Children with autism can demonstrate appropriate smiles. However, they may also use a "Cheshire cat" smile that doesn't cease and isn't used appropriately. The myth here is that individuals with autism don't express any emotion. Their anger and frustration are expressed via temper tantrums and behavioral outbursts. Facial expression may be restricted in individuals with autism; however, sometimes these individuals do smile and show other appropriate reactions.

3. Children with autism are not affectionate.

False. Children with autism experience the same emotions as other people, but their ways of expressing those emotions may be different. For example, many children with autism are tactile defensive. A hug can be a painfully aversive stimulus; consequently, a hug may not be a satisfying gesture for expressing affection. Affection can also be a very intimidating form of interaction to an individual with autism.

4. Autism can be outgrown.

False. If you are born with autism, you will die with autism, with very few exceptions. Autism does not go away, despite sensation-alized "cures" for autism in popular literature and talk shows. Many disabilities can mirror autistic symptoms, but not be autism. When these symptoms are "cured," the prudent action might be to re-diagnose the original disability — but that is rarely done. For example, the book *Fighting for Tony* by Mary Callahan (1987) discusses curing her son of autism by discovering cerebral allergies to dairy products. Despite the premise presented, Tony didn't have autism. He had cerebral allergies whose symptoms mirrored autism.

I have heard Temple Grandin, Ph.D., a high-functioning woman with autism, comment that she doesn't appreciate the term "cured." During an interview with Larry King, Temple noted that she may appear "cured" to him, but she has to deal with autism every minute of every day!

5. Children with autism are retarded.

True. This is a trick question! If you jumped to the conclusion, as most people do, that *retarded* means mental retardation, then the answer is *false*. Autism occurs on a continuum from high intelligence to low cognitive ability. The research literature suggests that mental retardation occurs in at least two-thirds of individuals with autism. However, *retardation* is defined as being delayed or behind in something. In autism, the area of social interaction is always retarded; the ability to understand and respond to social nuances is significantly delayed across the spectrum of the disorder. Social interaction is one of the key diagnostic components in differentiating autism from other disabilities.

6. Children with autism do not make eye contact.

False. Children with autism can make appropriate eye contact, but it is difficult for them. As professionals, we also become too focused on eye contact in isolation. I have reviewed numerous Individual Educational Plans and watched countless intervention sessions where someone was drilling eye contact by sitting and saying, "Look at me; you need to look at me." But the person wasn't engaged in any activity that required visual contact! A "normal" person doesn't demonstrate eye contact without a reason. Also, verbal individuals with autism have said it is easier to listen if they don't engage the visual channel; they find visual stimuli distracts from their ability to process auditory information. One little girl I worked with would ask if it was okay to look at the floor!

7. Children with autism do not relate to peers and adults.

False. Even though difficulty relating to people is a primary component of autism, it is not unusual to observe an immature level of interaction occurring. There is also a large difference between relating to peers versus adults. Adults follow polite rules of interaction and are a much safer interaction to attempt; children's spontaneity is intimidating and anxiety-provoking to a child with autism. Thus, interaction will often occur first with adults and have to be consciously developed with peers.

8. Children with autism cannot be tested by conventional means.

False. However, prior to intervention or educational programming, this statement is true. Children have to become comfortable with interacting and responding to presented stimuli before formal evaluation instruments will yield accurate results. Once accustomed to typical school procedures, many children eventually respond reliably to standardized measurements. A word of caution — results will be minimal estimates until probably mid-elementary school, even in high-functioning individuals. Modifications in test procedures can also result in more accurate test results.

9. Children with autism demonstrate behaviors that cannot be changed.

False. The behavioral component of autism is often one of the most frustrating areas for parents and professionals to cope with. While internal neurological needs may prompt many of the behaviors, these behaviors can be shaped and modified to less disruptive, socially inappropriate, or abusive behaviors. It is important to understand neurological aspects of behaviors when attempting to program through them — something which traditional behavior modification techniques overlook. Successful behavior modification is possible!

10. Maladaptive behaviors must be extinguished before remediation can begin.

False. If we waited to begin remediation until all maladaptive components had been extinguished, therapy would never start! Shaping maladaptive variables into less-problematic behaviors is a major aim of intervention goals. Years ago when I began working with autism as a speech-language pathologist, extinguishing echolalia was encouraged by putting a hand over your mouth (or the child's mouth). The intended message was "Don't echo"; the message received was "Don't talk." As a result, there was a generation of mute individuals with autism! Thankfully, we have since evolved to understand that it's not necessary to extinguish echolalia or any other undesirable behaviors; we just need to shape them into more acceptable ones.

11. Children with autism do not notice people or things in the environment.

False. Individuals with autism are often very astute in their perception of the environment, but don't respond as expected. They may miss what appears obvious to others and notice subtleties that others miss. Frequently, communication deficits interfere with the ability to share perceptions or reactions to the environment. It's not unusual to discover how much a child processed within an environment when he demonstrates memory for small details on a return visit.

12. Underneath the autism is a normal child, if you can discover the key.

False. "Cures" and "miracles" have contributed to this myth. In addition, the savant aspect of autism fuels the misperception among parents and professionals. "Idiot savant" refers to a person who has significantly impaired cognitive ability but a remarkable splinter skill. Savant components within autism are often evidenced in code systems, such as numeric calculations, calendar skills (e.g., providing the day of the week for any given date), and musical, artistic, or verbal reproduction. The important variable in savant skills is that most are a duplication of stimuli presented, not original, creative works. The autistic savant works much like a tape recorder or copy machine, reproducing something encountered. It is difficult, though, to stretch the savant skills to achieve functional creativity.

How did you do on the quiz? I hope some of these myths were explained well enough to disappear from your knowledge base. Now our focus can switch to building a new foundation of what autism is.

Definitions

Michael Powers, M.D., (1989) defines autism as a physical disorder of the brain causing a lifelong developmental disability. This definition provides an operational description that highlights the critical components of autism. Three aspects of his definition require further delineation.

First, it is a physical disorder of the brain. Powers states that the nature of the physical disorder is neurological and biochemical. The environment doesn't cause autism; parents don't cause autism; abuse doesn't cause autism. The brain is neurologically and biochemically different in the way it receives and responds to stimuli. The brain's capacity to attend, process, and assimilate information is triggered differently than through usual expectations. To think that intervention will result in a "normal" brain introduces a false assumption.

Second, autism is a lifelong disability. It is apparent in the individual from birth and will be present until death. Intervention will not cure autism or extinguish it. Throughout life, the individual will need to modify and cope with the disability.

Third, autism is a developmental disability. Onset is during the preschool years, or as various skills develop. The most frequently cited age for onset is between 30-36 months. Diagnosis may not be accomplished by that age, but a review of developmental milestones would indicate differences apparent by that time.

The most definitive medical definition for autism relies on the criteria delineated in *The Diagnostic and Statistical Manual of Mental Disorders, Fourth Edition (DSM-IV,* 1994), which also corresponds to the International Classification of Diseases. The *DSM-IV* specifies the minimum requirements for diagnosis of the autistic syndrome, presented in the chart on page 13.

The *DSM-IV* criteria clarify the four required components for a diagnosis of autism:

- impairment in social interaction
- impairment in communication
- restricted, repetitive, stereotyped patterns of behavior
- onset prior to age three

Diagnostic Criteria for Autistic Disorder

A. A total of 6 (or more) items from 1, 2, and 3, with at least two from 1, and one each from 2 and 3:

1. Qualitative impairment in social interaction, as manifested by at least two of the following:

    a. Marked impairments in the use of multiple nonverbal behaviors such as eye-to-eye gaze, facial expression, body postures, and gestures to regulate social interaction

    b. Failure to develop peer relationships appropriate to developmental level

    c. A lack of spontaneous seeking to share enjoyment, interests, or achievements with other people

    d. Lack of social or emotional reciprocity

2. Qualitative impairments in communication as manifested by at least one of the following:

    a. Delay in, or total lack of, the development of spoken language (not accompanied by an attempt to compensate through alternative modes of communication such as gesture and mime)

    b. In individuals with adequate speech, marked impairment in the ability to initiate or sustain a conversation with others

    c. Stereotyped and repetitive use of language or idiosyncratic language

    d. Lack of varied, spontaneous, make-believe play or social-imitative play appropriate to developmental level

3. Restricted repetitive and stereotyped patterns of behavior, interests, and activities, as manifested by at least one of the following:

    a. Encompassing preoccupation with one or more stereotyped and restricted patterns of interest that is abnormal either in intensity or focus

    b. Apparently inflexible adherence to specific, nonfunctional routines or rituals

    c. Stereotyped and repetitive motor mannerisms

    d. Persistent preoccupation with parts of objects

B. Delays or abnormal functioning in at least one of the following areas with onset prior to age three: (1) social interaction, (2) language as used in social communication, or (3) symbolic or imaginative play

C. The disturbance is not better accounted for by Rett's Disorder or Childhood Disintegrative Disorder.

Reprinted with permission from the *Diagnostic and Statistical Manual of Mental Disorders, Fourth Edition.* Copyright 1994 American Psychiatric Association.

All four of these primary pieces must be present for a diagnosis of autism. If one or two are missing, it is not autism; the disability just mirrors autistic characteristics. (Differential diagnosis among parallel disabilities is further discussed in Chapter 2.) The federal definition for autism is included in the *Individuals with Disabilities Act, P.L. 101-476, section 330.7 (b)(1):*

> "Autism" means a developmental disability significantly affecting verbal and nonverbal communication and social interaction, generally evident before age three, that adversely affects the child's educational performance.
>
> Other characteristics often associated with autism are:
>
> • engagement in repetitive activities and stereotyped movements
>
> • resistance to environmental change or change in daily routines
>
> • unusual response to sensory experiences
>
> The term does not apply if a child's educational performance is adversely affected primarily because the child has a serious emotional disturbance, as defined in paragraph (b) (9) of this section.

The primary diagnostic components of the federal definition are uniform with previous definitions. The important aspect here is the inclusion of autism as part of the *Individuals with Disabilities Education Act (IDEA),* an educational law. This definition places autism within the responsibilities of a multidisciplinary education team.

There are definite advantages and disadvantages to including autism within the educational realm. The primary disadvantage is that most educational professionals are not comfortable or familiar enough with autism to diagnose it confidently within the school setting. However, autism is a developmental disability, evidenced during early childhood. The diagnostic criteria components are based on observed behaviors. Education specialists are more likely to observe the behavioral symptoms of autism on a day-to-day basis than a physician during a routine office checkup. In addition, with the exception of child developmental disability clinics, the medical profession is further behind than education in recognizing and understanding autism. Many myths about autism remain strong in general medicine. The educational setting is struggling to cope with increased numbers of children with autism and autistic-like disorders. The reality of enrolled students with unique needs is forcing the education system to update quickly.

Facts about Autism

Prevalent summary facts and figures about autism are listed in the chart on page 15. Aspects of this information are addressed during later portions of this book, but a few explanatory comments are offered here.

Autism Facts

- **Prevalence**

  Third most common developmental disability

      15 per 10,000 births

- **Gender Ratio**

  Higher incidence in males

      2.6 males to 1 female at low end

      4.1 males to 1 female at high end

- **IQ**

  $2/3$ to $3/4$ have cognitive impairment (i.e., IQ below 70)

- **Primary Symptoms**

  Occur on a continuum from mild to severe

  Communication

      40% are mute/nonverbal/apraxic

      Echolalia

      Monotone

      Jargon

      Delays and differences

  Social Interaction

      Abnormal relationships

      Difficulty relating to self, environment, other people

  Stereotyped Behaviors

      Rituals and routines

      Insistence on sameness

  Abnormal Sensory Responses

      Hypersensitive

      Hyposensitive

  Present at Birth

The literature suggests that, in the vast majority of individuals with autism, mental retardation is a dominant piece of the syndrome. The literature, however, is probably negatively skewed for two reasons. First, lower-functioning individuals within the autistic spectrum are identified consistently, while higher-functioning individuals are often missed or misdiagnosed as learning disabled, language disabled, or "weird." Second, the previous *DSM* criteria were very restrictive in allowing diagnosis for the milder end of the autistic continuum, resulting in milder- and higher-functioning individuals not being able to meet the diagnostic criteria for labeling.

My own experience suggests an increase in more normal-functioning individuals within the autistic disorder. Higher-functioning individuals are beginning to receive the label, which should result in modifying the negative severity of the current statistics on IQ.

Data on communication within autism suggests that apraxia may be part of the syndrome in almost half of the individuals. *Praxis* means the ability to motor program; the prefix *a* introduces a lack of or difficulty in the ability to program speech. Consequently, the individuals with autism who are nonverbal are not mute by choice, but rather as part of the neurological aspect of the syndrome.

Echolalia is the immediate or delayed imitation of verbally-presented stimuli, a high-frequency characteristic in autism. Other speech characteristics include the use of a personal, nonsensical language (jargon) and a lack of verbal inflection and vocal variety (monotone). General communication development (e.g., phonology, the development of sounds) will evidence simple delays accompanied by unusual language differences (e.g., echolalia).

Impaired social interaction in relating to the world is a very dramatic and noticeable characteristic of autism. The children's lack of relating to the environment usually results in concerns for their safety. For example, these children don't realize that they might get hurt if they let go while swinging on the monkey bars. Difficulty relating to others is often evidenced through confusion in pronouns and gender terms, such as *Mrs./Mr.* or *he/she*. These terms are too abstract. The individual with autism prefers to use proper names, even when referring to herself, to keep the reference concrete.

Sensory system differences are a major part of the neurological and bio-chemical aspects of the disorder. An individual with autism might be hypersensitive to some sensory stimuli, while hyposensitive to other sensory stimuli. The confusion for families and professionals is the variability within the sensory systems. On a good chemical day, a child may not be hypersensitive to auditory noises, but on another day, the child may be very upset by them. A child may be hypersensitive to some auditory stimuli (e.g., bells and sirens) but hyposensitive to other types of auditory stimuli (e.g., the human voice).

Sensory system differences can account for many of the behaviors which puzzle professionals trying to develop appropriate programs for children. For example, many individuals with autism are picky eaters. It is quite likely, however, that the oral cavity (which is very sensitive) just cannot tolerate certain tastes, smells, and textures, resulting in what appears to be manipulative behavior.

Stereotyped behaviors confound and amaze parents and professionals. The individual with autism imposes a routine that sometimes only he understands, but it is critical to comply with his sense of order. These routines are an anxiety-control characteristic; a way to make sense of the world and limit intimidating new features. Routines can serve as the professional's best friend or worst enemy — more on that later!

Summary Comments

Basic plus additional pieces typically complete an individual's autism puzzle. The additional variables are supplemental to the core symptoms. The challenge is to sort out the individual pieces of the puzzle, examine the size and configuration of each piece, and determine how they all fit together. One piece may have a profound impact or influence on another characteristic, or have no effect at all. But the severity of the pieces is part of the diagnostic puzzle. If the puzzle is not put together carefully, intervention success will be minimized. The relationship among the autistic puzzle pieces must be the deciding factor in determining appropriate goals for intervention.

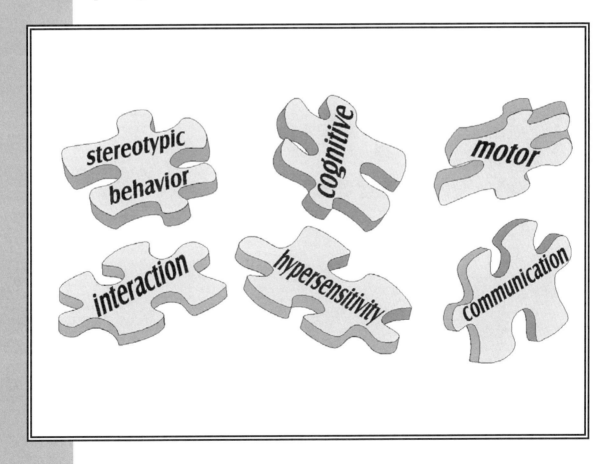

In summary, an eclectic, working definition of autism is:

➡ Autism is a syndrome/spectrum disorder.

➡ Autism has four major diagnostic criteria which must be present:

- impairment in social interaction
- impairment in communication
- restricted, repetitive, stereotyped patterns of behavior
- onset prior to age three

➡ A variety of other characteristics may complete the syndrome's puzzle.

➡ The syndrome aspect of autism results in the unique individuality of the disability; each person's syndrome puzzle is different, even though common pieces exist.

➡ The symptoms of autism occur on a continuum from mild to severe.

Chapter 2
Diagnosis of Autism

Even though autism is a neurological disorder, it is still diagnosed by observing a child's behavior.

Temple Grandin
Thinking in Pictures

Medical vs. Educational Diagnosis

Wouldn't it be wonderful if we could conduct medical evaluations that would diagnose autism definitively for an individual? Unfortunately, science hasn't yet arrived at that state of knowledge. One of my seven-year-old clients was undergoing extensive chemical analysis as part of a diagnostic evaluation and had to provide several urine samples over the course of three days. When the doctor asked if she had any questions before they left, she asked, "Are you going to see autism in my pee?" We wish it were that easy!

Definitions for the diagnosis of autistic disorder continue to be based on descriptive observation. That places the burden of responsibility for keen, careful clinical impressions on the part of parents and professionals. The previous chapter cited the inclusion of autism as part of the *Individuals with Disabilities Act*, which assigns educational settings responsibility in diagnosis. The most critical task is determining the primary disability, and then differentiating secondary components of the syndrome.

The diagnosis of autism is not an exact science. One of the continuing debates is medical vs. educational diagnosis of the autistic spectrum disorder. While some would prefer to leave diagnosis of autism in the medical arena, medical science prefers definitive, measurable evidence of disorders. The opportunity to observe behavior in various settings with a variety of people and activities is not a luxury afforded within many medical settings. The educational setting provides a consistent environment in which professionals can observe and analyze a child's behaviors and skills over time.

Misdiagnosis is often voiced as one of the greatest fears within the educational setting. The possibility of inaccurate diagnosis also exists, and occurs, within the medical profession. A misdiagnosis of stomach cancer for what was actually gall bladder is a welcome shift in diagnosis, but calling the disorder an ulcer when it is really cancer can result in dire consequences. But it happens. Diagnosis within a medical arena can be wrong. When discovered, the accurate diagnosis is introduced and intervention altered accordingly.

Within the educational setting, the same principle applies. A team meets to share and compare impressions to determine the primary disability. Based on available data, the team reaches a conclusion to the best of their collective experience. If that conclusion is inaccurate or wrong, several procedures are in place to ensure opportunities to re-evaluate the accuracy of a label. The team reconvenes minimally once a year and can call a meeting anytime the need arises. The multidisciplinary team conducts a complete re-evaluation every three years to collect new data and impressions to determine if diagnosis, placement, and intervention goals continue to be appropriate. There are more required safeguards within special education provisions to guarantee re-evaluation of labels than in the medical setting.

Why does special education law require consistent team meetings? Because labels change, based on intervention and new impressions by multiple staff over time. It is not necessarily a sign of incompetence to alter a label, but rather a sign of competence and provision of appropriate services. The goal of some disability labels, such as a developmental phonological disorder, is to provide remediation which results in the label being dropped as no longer accurate; the problem has been resolved. Some disabilities, such as cognitive impairments, become more apparent over time as the yardstick to measure skills increases.

Professionals within the educational setting need to assume responsibility to educate themselves to diagnose autism and other developmental disorders. Educational professionals would not send a child to a physician to differentiate a learning disability or to determine the functioning within a cognitive deficit, such as educable mentally impaired vs. trainable mentally impaired. Autism is a developmental disorder that is diagnosed through observation of interactions, skills, and responses to stimuli. Educational professionals are trained to evaluate academic skills and determine developmental levels.

I am not advocating that multidisciplinary teams suddenly presume expertise in diagnosing autism. I am, though, encouraging educational personnel to attend workshops and in-service presentations, read current literature, and refine their observation skills. Forging a comfort level within childhood developmental disabilities through experience will increase the likelihood of a team member raising the label of autism for discussion in a multidisciplinary staffing. Discussion and debate are healthy vehicles to insure consideration of all options. Chapter 4 further develops the role and responsibility of various team members in the evaluation and intervention process.

Utopia would combine the expertise of both education and medicine. Some families and professionals are fortunate enough to have a multi-disciplinary clinic or team located near them as a resource; others must struggle for years to find a professional who recognizes the symptoms of autism and can assist in programming to meet its unique needs.

Differential Diagnosis

Following a recent presentation, a parent told me that autism is now equivalent to a designer label — it's *the* disability to have — the "in" thing! After I thought about the comment, there is some truth in the statement. *Autism* has become the preschool label heard most often, even when I feel strongly the disability evidenced is *not* autism. Several child disability clinics attach the label of autism whenever they observe a neurological profile which includes any self-stimulatory characteristics or pragmatic/social deficits in a child. The minimal diagnostic criteria delineated in the *DSM-IV* are not uniformly applied across settings. I don't want *autism* to become a generic term when nothing else can be determined, but I believe, in some areas of the country, that is already happening.

Differential diagnosis is an important step in determining the primary disability and subsequent programming. However, because autism is a developmental disorder and diagnosis is based on behavioral observation, the diagnostic criteria leave room for individual interpretation.

Another factor that contributes to confusion in diagnosis is co-morbidity, as when autism occurs in conjunction with another disability, such as deafness, blindness, or cerebral palsy. The differentiation blurs even further when autism occurs with another developmental disorder, such as attention deficit disorder or a learning disability. Even though the diagnostic challenge increases in cases of co-morbidity, it is critical to differentiate the primary and secondary factors of the disability. The attention problems that are part of an autism syndrome will be treated differently than a true attention deficit disorder. Once again, the intervention will only be as effective as the accuracy in diagnosis.

A third factor to consider is confusion in disability terminology. Many preschool children are diagnosed with pervasive developmental disorder, or PDD, which displays itself like autism. Over time, parents and teachers have come to believe PDD *is* autism; that they are synonymous terms. Autism and PDD are *NOT* synonyms, but exist on a similar continuum of diagnostic categories. To explain differential diagnosis, an overview explanation of the *Diagnostic and Statistical Manual of Mental Disorders, Fourth Edition (DSM-IV)* is presented here.

The *DSM-IV* (1994) is a multiaxial system for differentiating disorders. This explanation will focus on Axis I, which defines Clinical Disorders. The ten major categories of Clinical Disorders included in Axis I of the *DSM-IV* are:

Mental Retardation
Learning Disorders
Motor Skills Disorders
Communication Disorders
Pervasive Developmental Disorders
Attention Deficit and Disruptive Behavior Disorders
Feeding and Eating Disorders of Infancy or Early Childhood
Tic Disorders
Elimination Disorders
Other Disorders of Infancy, Childhood, or Adolescence

Each umbrella category is further divided into subcategories that have specific diagnostic criteria. For Pervasive Developmental Disorders (PDD), the subcategories include:

1. Autistic Disorder

2. Rett's Disorder

3. Childhood Disintegrative Disorder

4. Asperger's Disorder

5. Pervasive Developmental Disorder - Not Otherwise Specified

All five of the above PDD subcategories share a common set of characteristics: poor social skills, communication deficits, stereotyped behaviors, and early onset. The diagnostic challenge is to differentiate which subcategory best accounts for the behavioral profile. (Note, too, that there are other diagnostic options under different Axis I Clinical Disorder subcategory terms, such as PICA, Stereotyped Movement Disorder, Mental Impairment, Attention Deficit Disorder, as well as under Axis II and III, such as Childhood Schizophrenia or Fragile X Syndrome.)

Most professionals can place a child within the PDD category based on characteristics observed. The next diagnostic step is crucial to consider carefully — discriminating which PDD subcategory describes the child's disability the best. The five subcategories differ subtly in how and when the key characteristics show themselves. The chart below lists some of these differences.

Pervasive Developmental Disorders (PDD)

Autism Disorder

- Impairment in social interaction

- Impairment in communication

- Restricted, repetitive, stereotyped patterns of behavior

- Onset prior to age three

Rett's Disorder

- Normal prenatal and perinatal developmental period until at least five months of age. Between five and 48 months, onset of the PDD profile occurs, but with a few differences:

    Deceleration in head circumference

    Stereotyped hand movements increase to constant, non-functional hand-wringing

    Poor motor coordination for trunk and walking movements

- Significant speech-language problems with an impaired motor component

- Almost exclusively a female disorder

Childhood Disintegrative Disorder

- At least two years of normal development in all areas (i.e., verbal and nonverbal communication, social relationships, play, adaptive behavior) before onset of a clinically-significant loss of previously-acquired skills. The residual deficits then match the characteristic PDD profile.

Asperger's Disorder

- Requires only two major diagnostic pieces to be present:

    Qualitative impairment in social interaction

    Restricted, repetitive, stereotyped patterns of behavior, interests, and activities

- No significant delays in language, cognitive development, self-help skills, or adaptive behavior

Pervasive Developmental Disorder - Not Otherwise Specified (PDD-NOS)

- Profile best fits under the PDD major heading of Axis I, but doesn't meet the criteria for one of the four subcategories above

Accurate differential diagnosis is essential to avoid misleading assumptions in remediation plans and prognosis for the future. For example, a child may evidence all the characteristics of PDD when very young and prior to any formal intervention. The child's social skills, however, may reflect a lack of confidence more than aloneness or actual isolation. In that case, a diagnosis of PDD-NOS may insure a neurological approach to intervention while deferring the long-term label until remedial programming has been in place for a few years. Often an initial diagnosis of PDD-NOS will change major category headings to become a learning disability, a communication disorder, or an attention deficit disorder by early elementary school. In other words, the primary disability may be refined with programming and a more subtle, yet specific disorder may become apparent.

The umbrella label of PDD is frequently used as a diagnostic option for young preschool children. This option allows the child to receive a label in the appropriate category heading, but defers differential diagnosis into a subcategory until the child has benefitted from intense intervention, modification, and neurological maturation. But using the PDD label can cause confusion if the profile meets autistic criteria and is not labeled as such. Professionals need to make every attempt to complete differential diagnosis by early elementary school to optimize children's educational programming.

Differential diagnosis requires experience with a wide range of childhood developmental disorders. Observing behaviors in children over time is very different from simply matching up a child with behavioral profiles in a book, specifically the *DSM-IV*.

It is also important to retain the concept of a syndrome or spectrum disorder. At a staffing which I attended, school personnel listed communication deficits, impaired social skills, sensory-motor deficits, stereotyped behaviors, and mental impairment each as separate disabilities! They did not want to acknowledge or accept the label of autism, so each piece of the syndrome's definition was listed as if it occurred independently from the others. Differential diagnosis must define the major disability and then discriminate the adjunct syndrome components.

Educational Diagnosis — Quadrant Theory

Once a diagnosis of autism has been made, further evaluation of a child's functional ability is necessary for placement and programming within an educational setting. Autism occurs across an extreme spectrum, from very high functioning (e.g., Asperger's Disorder) to very low functioning.

The label of autism alone should not determine educational placement. Other factors must be added to the puzzle in making decisions for educational potential.

The University of Iowa Child Psychiatric Services proposed a model (1983) based on experience placing and developing educational programming for children over many years. The model uses two factors as the keys for prognosis — communication and intelligence. Using verbal vs. nonverbal communication as the horizontal axis and high vs. low IQ as the vertical axis, four diagnostic subgroups result that assist in educational planning. (An IQ of 60 is used to indicate a high level of cognitive functioning because this implies measurement early in programming. If a preschool child attains a measurable IQ of 60, he will most probably demonstrate normal to high IQ eventually.) This premise, called the Quadrant Theory, is illustrated below.

Diagnostic Subgroups of Autism and Educational Placement

	Fluent/Verbal Speech	Nonverbal
High IQ	**I** Regular/Aide	**II** Regular/Aide
↑ 60	LD	LD
	EMH	EMH
	III BD	**IV** BD
↓ 60	TMH	TMH
Low IQ	Severe/Profound	Severe/Profound

Subgroup I: High IQ and Verbal

- This group is synonymous with high-functioning autism and includes individuals with Asperger's Disorder.

- Behaviors and self-stimulation are minimal in this group. Abusive or socially inappropriate characteristics are usually not evidenced or extinguish early.

- This group includes precocious readers (by two or three years old) and memorizers; often misdiagnosed as hyperlexic.

- Visual skills are strong.

- Strong ritualistic tendencies and obsessive-compulsive traits. Individuals can also demonstrate peculiar and intense interests.

- May be passive or bizarre in social situations. High IQ results in an awareness of social pressure; the anxiety results in total withdrawal (passive) or extreme acting out (bizarre).

- Individuals may become aware of their differences as they mature, but be unable to generate alternative behaviors to fit in.

Subgroup II — High IQ and Nonverbal

- Large gap between verbal and performance IQ.

- May be hypersensitive to auditory stimuli.

- Self-stimulation and behavior are minimal in intensity.

- Very strong visual skills; these individuals watch intensely.

- Aloof, silent, isolated type of autism; individuals tune out easily.

- Individuals can be manipulative and stubborn.

- Good candidates for augmentative or alternative forms of communication.

Subgroup III — Low IQ and Verbal

- Individuals display the worst behavior within autism; screamers and yellers who generate noise louder than what is present in the environment. Can become aggressive as they get older.

- Rote, echolalia, and perseveration in speech. A lot of non-meaningful speech present, which can be deceptive.

- High frequency and intensity of self-stimulatory behaviors.

- Poor attention.

Subgroup IV — Low IQ and Nonverbal

- Individuals are mute, using few words or signs.

- High interest in mechanical things.

- Hypersensitivity to auditory stimuli.

- Self-stimulation socially inappropriate and often abusive.

- Individuals don't relate to people.

In addition to a resulting behavioral profile, the Quadrant Theory assists in educational placement. In general, the high IQ groups (Subgroups I and II) should be accommodated in regular classrooms. Individual aides may be necessary to insure classroom modifications to meet their needs. As the IQ level approximates the range of 70-80, a smaller classroom with increased individual instruction might be beneficial, such as a learning disability resource, cross-categorical, communication disordered, or educable mentally impaired classroom. Subgroup II students may need to begin in a smaller classroom until a communication system can be established to respond to information requested, but a regular class-room should be the goal.

Subgroups III and IV will probably require special education placement and benefit from smaller, individualized instruction. Classroom options include low-level educable mentally impaired, behavior disordered, train-able mentally impaired, and severe/profound classrooms. Placement should be consistent with the student's cognitive level and teaching should be functional, incorporating a concrete, multimodality approach. Placement options are discussed further in Chapter 4, Team Coordina-tion and Responsibilities.

Reasons for Diagnosis

No one ever enjoys suggesting a disability label to a parent or individual, regardless of the circumstances. At times, diagnosis is avoided in an attempt not to upset someone emotionally. Even though the task of explaining a disability is not pleasant, ethically, it needs to be done. It is professionally irresponsible to avoid using a label if consensus has been reached on the disability. The following case example illustrates the point.

An Ohio family moved to Illinois for the husband's new position. Their youngest son had been enrolled in an Early Childhood Program. The receiving school contacted Ohio school personnel to determine the child's primary needs prior to receipt of records. The Ohio teachers all discussed the child's "autism" and "autistic characteristics" for which they were programming. When the child arrived for his first day of school in Illinois, the staff met the parents in the hall to welcome them and assure them that the teachers had experience with autism and were looking forward to working with their son. At this point, the mother burst into tears; the father furiously told them they were crazy and headed for the door with his son and wife; the school personnel were bewildered.

After everyone calmed down and the principal sorted things out, the problem became quite clear. The preschool in Ohio knew that the child's disability was autism, programmed with autism in mind, but didn't want to label the child as having autism. In Early Childhood, a label of speech-language delayed was routinely used for all enrolled students. So while the school operated under an assumption, it was never shared or even suggested to the parents. The friendly greeting in Illinois had dropped a bombshell for which the parents had no warning or time to prepare.

These parents sought an independent evaluation and accepted the label when it was responsibly and sensitively presented to them with observational data to support it. They didn't enjoy hearing "autism," but they accepted that their son met the diagnostic criteria when it was explained with anecdotal impressions. Further exploration of sharing diagnostic results with families is shared in Chapter 10, Home Intervention.

Why is diagnosis so important? If the behavioral characteristics are so unusual, they will be noticed and programmed for, right?

I would like to agree. For lower-functioning individuals within the autism syndrome, the previous statement is relatively true. However, higher-functioning and milder cases are often the ones missed, for a variety of reasons. The problem is, mild higher-functioning individuals have a better prognosis for maximizing their capabilities and achieving functional independence if their disorder is modified. Yet they are the individuals routinely missed, compromising their chances for success. Another case of missed diagnosis further supports the importance of diagnosis, even in high-functioning individuals.

A college freshman was referred by a dorm counselor for evaluation. The young man had been the subject of harassment and teasing in the dorms, but the dorm counselor felt there was more to these problems than just a "weird" student. The student was 19 years old and had been followed by a major medical clinic throughout his first 12 years of school. His mother had died when he was young and his father was coping as well as possible. The young man had graduated with honors from his high school and had above a 3.0 grade-point average (4.0 scale) for his first semester of college. He had classic autism — very poor social skills; mechanical-sounding speech; poor hygiene; no awareness or ability to read subtle nuances in social interaction; very ritualistic behaviors, like rocking back and forth when anxious; and a bald, bloody spot where he had been pulling out his hair. He was like a frightened rabbit or deer in the headlights, trying to cope independently on a college campus. His sole focus was studying, which he did all day and night. His social skills were like those of a young grade-school child.

Follow-up revealed the young man's awareness of "differences" throughout his life, but no one wanted to label him because he was so bright. People felt that labeling him would be a disservice. The result was that he received no special services to modify autistic characteristics. Here was an extremely bright young man who didn't know the basics about coping with independent life. His excellent potential was critically compromised because of appearances.

The first issue to address is discriminating lower- and higher-functioning individuals within the syndrome. The Quadrant Theory offers a way to differentiate within the autism continuum for school placement and programming. The critical variables for educational prognosis are communication abilities and intelligence.

Dr. Luke Tsai, University of Michigan Medical Center, identified four reasons for differentiating between high- and low-functioning autism in a paper presented at the 1990 Annual Conference of the Autism Society of America:

1. High-functioning individuals miss early diagnosis.

2. Schools often refuse to identify high-functioning individuals as having autism.

3. Schools often misdiagnose high-functioning autism, resulting in services which don't meet the individual's needs.

4. Facilities and placement options for low-functioning autism are not appropriate for high-functioning individuals.

Individuals who are severely involved within autism will be identified for special services. Higher-functioning individuals who can handle academic assignments but who have difficulty relating to people are more likely to be overlooked. The more "normal" the academic performance, the more hesitancy toward a special education label. Many administrators believe the heavy label of autism is too emotional to place on a normally achieving student, regardless of social or interaction skills. The lack of an early label results in missed services. A child with the intellectual capability to learn how to model appropriate social behavior quickly and modify through components of the disability, is not given that chance.

The higher-functioning individual with autism may be misdiagnosed as having a behavior disorder, a learning disability, or an attention deficit disorder. Assumptions may be made, based on an erroneous label, that the student is willfully choosing to misbehave or not pay attention. The services provided may not address the actual syndrome components at all; the services might punish the student for something he doesn't understand and can't control.

Reticence to diagnose autism in some schools may be based on limited resources. The "autism classroom" might be designed for cognitively-impaired individuals with a nonverbal teaching emphasis. Administrators often feel if a label is assigned to a student, there must be a corresponding classroom for placement. Higher-functioning individuals do not require a special classroom, only special modifications and services.

A normal to high IQ within the autistic spectrum greatly improves prognosis. Dr. Tsai highlighted the following seven differences between high IQ and low IQ autism:

1. IQ "increases" over time.

The IQ doesn't actually increase, but becomes more measurable. Intelligence evaluation is based on question and response between an individual and the examiner. The person with autism can be very anxious in that setting and accuracy is compromised, resulting in minimal estimates for several years.

One client was non-testable in preschool (which usually indicates mental impairment), achieved an IQ score of 60 in first grade (educable mentally impaired range), and attained an IQ of 130 in fourth grade. Her IQ did not change that significantly — her ability to demonstrate her IQ for the school in a testing situation is what changed over time.

2. Autistic symptoms reduce over time.

As a higher-functioning individual becomes comfortable in various environments, he adapts to the setting and relaxes. Self-stimulatory behaviors and the intensity of bizarre behaviors decrease significantly over time. The educational setting provides a constructive, focused channel for energy and overflow behaviors diminish.

3. Social responses are less deviant.

Pragmatic communication, the use of language in various social contexts, is one of the core symptoms of autism. Programming can directly teach appropriate social interaction skills and appeal to the higher intellect to modify significantly deviant responses. Teaching subtle social nuances is more difficult with lower intelligence and usually requires patterned modeling over many trials to accomplish change in social responses.

4. Language problems are less severe.

Language is a code system that requires a certain level of cognitive competence to master. Basic language development is generally intact in high-IQ individuals with autism due to extensive modeling and echolalic practice. The more abstract components of language can then be directly taught in intervention.

5. Behavioral components are less severe.

Autism means aloneness or self. The high-functioning individual with autism often goes into a cognitive self-stimulation to create a world that is calming and enjoyable. The lower-functioning individual is more likely to require physical self-stimulation to calm down or relax. Consequently, higher-IQ individuals with autism are not as likely to demonstrate socially inappropriate or self-abusive behaviors.

6. There is a lower rate of seizure disorders.

Higher intellectual functioning usually suggests less global brain damage or significant differences. Consequently, a more intact brain has less likelihood of misfiring neurologically with seizures.

7. Educational performance is more normal.

Normal to high cognitive potential should result in fairly normal academic functioning. Teaching style will have an impact on achievement, but generally the high IQ individual with autism will do well in school, particularly in concrete subjects.

Summary Comments

➡ Autism occurs on a continuum of severity.

➡ The behavioral profile of the disorder shares features with several other disabilities. Careful differential diagnosis is critical to insure appropriate, focused intervention.

➡ An incorrect diagnosis or assumption may prevent an individual from receiving intensive intervention within the optimal early years.

➡ Differential diagnosis is not an easy task! Discriminating subtle differences within disabilities requires reliable reports from parents and caregivers, careful observations, experience across a variety of disabilities, and comparison of behavioral characteristics across settings and people. The next chapter discusses the key characteristics of autism for focused observation.

Chapter 3
Characteristics of Autism

The brain is made up of many different parts, containing many different abilities. Just because one area is affected doesn't mean others are too. . . . The ability of the brain to compensate for damage by using functions that are still intact is often overlooked.

Donna Williams
Somebody Somewhere

Skill Development

The child with symptoms of autism is likely to stand out in a group of children rather easily. The characteristics are different, often bizarre, and tend to intimidate the uninformed public. While a child may appear attractive and "normal," the child's behavioral characteristics, triggered in response to sensory stimuli in the environment, set him apart immediately. Unfortunately, these bizarre differences can overshadow intact abilities that may also be present.

Compounding the issue, autism is a developmental disorder whose diagnosis relies on careful behavioral observation. The pattern of symptoms needs to fit a defined characteristic profile to result in attachment of a label. Observation to discriminate the "differences" sometimes overlooks the strengths in a zealous attempt to be accountable to the disability components.

The relationship between the development of specific skills can also provide insight to the relationship of strengths and weaknesses in a child's syndrome components. While cognitive development has the greatest impact on development of other skills, the measurement of cognitive ability is often difficult to ascertain in a child with autism. Generally high skills in all other areas accompanied by low measurement of cognitive skills might suggest better cognitive ability than what is demonstrated in formal evaluation. However, an impression of high cognitive skill that is not substantiated by any other skill performance should be re-evaluated.

Therefore, one level of observation should be to observe carefully to gain an impression of skill development. Skills can be grouped in several ways, but one example is to group skill development with typical academic categories, such as motor development (gross motor and fine motor), adaptive behavior (self-help; independence), communication (verbal and nonverbal), cognitive, and social. A "normal" child's skill performance is graphed in Diagram A below, followed by a low-functioning child with autism (Diagram B) and a high-functioning child with autism (Diagram C). A discussion of the major differences follows.

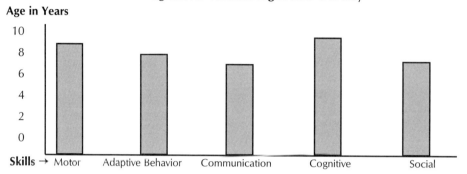

Diagram A: Normal Eight-Year-Old Boy

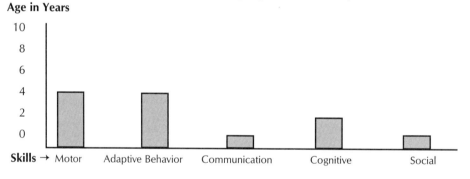

Diagram B: Low-Functioning Eight-Year-Old Boy with Autism

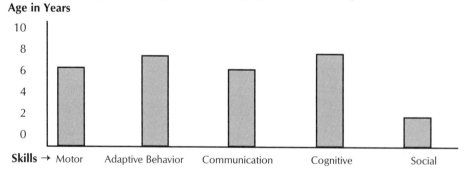

Diagram C: High-Functioning Eight-Year-Old Boy with Autism

Diagram A illustrates fairly consistent skills across all categories, commensurate with chronological age expectations for a normal eight-year-old. Since the subject is male, research suggests the possibility of slight delays in communication and social skills.

Diagram B illustrates an autistic boy with fairly severe cognitive impairment, functioning at approximately a three-year-old level. Notice that this child's motor skills actually exceed his cognitive skills, as do his adaptive skills. It is not unusual to observe a discrepancy between motor skills and cognitive skills with motor skills developing more age appropriately. However, there continues to be a significant discrepancy from chronological age for all skills measured.

Diagram C illustrates a skill sample chart for a high-functioning autistic male. Cognitive skills are the highest on this boy's chart, with adaptive behavior rating very close. High-functioning individuals may tend to try to control and manipulate the world to ease their anxiety, resulting in strong independence. This child's communication and motor skills are just slightly delayed as compared to his cognitive skills. Social skills demonstrate the largest gap in this boy's skill development as compared to his cognitive potential.

When autism is present, there is a significant discrepancy in social skills as compared to other skills. Abnormal social interaction is one of the primary diagnostic criteria for autism, regardless of functioning level. Except in cases of a severe apraxia (nonverbal) isolated type autism, social will remain the lowest of a child's skills. This profile varies from that of mentally-impaired children without an autism component. For example, most children with Down Syndrome are very social and affectionate. Social skill development is determined by the nature of the disability's characteristics, not by the level of cognitive functioning.

These three samples illustrated are not intended to serve as the model or as an exact guideline for low- or high-functioning skill profiles. The diagrams provide a visual example of one way to chart data objectively for comparison. Listing a variety of skills should also call attention to a combination of both strengths and weaknesses in the child's profile rather than concentrating only on differences.

There are other ways to organize skill observation data for analysis. Some professionals group strengths and weaknesses in sensory-modality channels, such as auditory-to-verbal stimuli compared to visual-to-verbal stimuli. An example might be the individual who names objects presented visually, but does not respond to verbal directions or requests. Another method is the *Gilliam Autism Rating Scale* (1995), which summarizes observational data into four major areas: stereotyped behaviors, communication, social interaction, and general development. The composite scores yield an autism quotient that suggests the probability of the presence of autism (see Appendix 3C, page 52).

The important point is to group observation data into larger categories which highlight both capabilities and disabilities across applied skill areas.

Specific Characteristics

Composite skill performance is compiled from observing specific characteristics and then grouping them into major categories for summary impressions. Anxiety about making a diagnosis through informal observation is often due to being unsure which characteristics are salient features of the autistic syndrome. Despite many professionals' anxiety about diagnosis based on informal observation, many of the critical behaviors characteristic of autism are observed readily within an educational setting.

It is important that the professional conducting observational analysis be removed from the responsibility of conducting an activity for the entire class. The professional's focus should not be split between an activity and the child being observed; such distraction would minimize awareness of the often subtle behaviors of autism.

Specific observational data should address the four major diagnostic criteria delineated in the *DSM-IV*, while also determining other supplemental aspects of the syndrome.

A sample of high-frequency, salient, behavioral characteristics for autism are listed below and explained in the following section with examples of ways to observe these characteristics. Specific strategies for dealing with the characteristics follow in subsequent chapters.

Characteristics of Autism to Note During Focused Observation

1. Withdrawal
2. Poor Reality Contact
3. Delayed or Splintered Motor Development
4. Self-Stimulation
5. Splintered Perceptual Skills
6. Perseveration
7. Echolalia
8. Poor Identity Concept
9. Ritualism
10. Mental Rigidity
11. Attention Deficit
12. Impaired Social Interaction
13. Mechanical Movement and/or Speech
14. Perimeter Walking

---

1. Withdrawal

Most preschoolers are excited about communicating or playing with other children and toys in a new setting. It is usually quite apparent to the casual observer, therefore, when preschoolers physically isolate themselves within the classroom. Young children tend to participate *en masse*, so a lone figure becomes fairly obvious. Part of the child's withdrawal may also show a lack of awareness or interest for what is occurring within the environment. An extremely shy child observes situations passively and very carefully, whereas a child with autism appears oblivious to the environment and does his own thing. The child's behavior appears self-absorbed on chosen activities or demonstrates an intense internal focus.

2. Poor Reality Contact

Many children with autism are referred initially for an audiometric evaluation with questions about hearing ability, due to extremely poor reality contact. A child wandering within a setting with little or no reaction to auditory stimulation is noticeable to a classroom observer. Withdrawal has been noted at a level in which there is no response or reaction to environmental stimuli; only internal stimuli trigger a response. Little or no awareness to people or activities denotes the stereotyped picture of autism — children isolated within themselves, oblivious to the world around them.

3. Delayed or Splintered Motor Development

Motor development follows Piagetian stages of development, parallel with cognitive and neurological development. The unifying factor is interaction. Most infants are stimulated neurologically to seek their bottle, favorite toy, or comfort from a caregiver. That emotional need for interaction spurs motor development. The first stage of cognitive development is called sensorimotor, in which a child problem solves by acting motorically upon a problem. Autism often results in motor delay due to the lack of reciprocal interaction and awareness which triggers the desire for motor response.

Motor delays can be evidenced in both gross- and fine-motor development, and these delays may be uneven or splintered. A child who displays excellent balance, climbing, running, and spinning may not be able to manipulate a paper and pencil to write her name. A child with keen manual fine-motor dexterity might not be able to coordinate oral fine-motor control for speech. Some children with autism are incredibly coordinated and gifted in motor skills. Thus, uneven skills can be very apparent in the area of motor development.

Involving physical therapy and occupational therapy professionals in the evaluation process is important due to the high incidence of motor delays within the syndrome of autism. The lack of response to typical environment stimulation often necessitates a more direct exercise therapeutic approach for developing fine- and gross-motor skills for these children.

4. Self-Stimulation

Self-stimulation is rhythmic, repetitive, motor movement which provides pleasurable stimulation. Typical examples within the autistic spectrum are hand flapping, finger flicking, rocking, and circling movements. Self-stimulation ranges in severity and type from fairly mild characteristics to socially inappropriate (e.g., masturbation) and severely self-abusive behaviors. These self-stimulatory behaviors are usually easily observed due to their frequency, intensity, and unusual, repetitive characteristics.

Self-stimulatory behaviors usually occur when a child's autistic world is intruded upon and external stimuli become overwhelming or anxiety provoking. Introducing new people, routines, or materials may trigger self-stimulatory movements. Self-stimulatory behaviors are often used by the child with autism to calm down by generating a self-controlled, repetitive stimulus. Self-stimulatory characteristics of autism and strategies for shaping and modifying them will be addressed more specifically in Chapter 7, Behavior Management and Chapter 8, Classroom Strategies.

5. Splintered Perceptual Skills

Various combinations of sensory-perceptual skills can be splintered in unique strengths or weaknesses among children with autism. For example, the visual-motor perceptions involved in a three-dimensional shape ball were completed easily with no trial-and-error mistakes by a three-year-old during an evaluation. His mother assured the teachers that he had not played with one of the shape balls prior to the evaluation. Another child could not visually see that a shape would fit the appropriate-sized hole, even when the examiner provided hand-over-hand assistance.

Sensory perception of stimuli is often different in individuals with autism. Donna Williams (*Somebody Somewhere,* 1994) vividly described her visual-perception difficulties in trying to assimilate visual stimuli into a meaningful picture. Her acute visual sensitivity resulted in seeing images as microscopic dust particles floating in front of her eyes as a splintered prism of colors. The larger visual image was not apparent because she was so distracted by the visual patterns. In *Nobody Nowhere* (1992), Donna described auditory stimuli as patterned sound that was fascinating to listen to, but had no meaning within the structured sound units of words and sentences. Perceptual differences can also be observed through unique mannerisms a child with autism might demonstrate when interacting with materials. For example, some children hold objects to the side of their faces and use peripheral vision to scan them. The eye-hand coordination required to complete puzzles is another example of an observable skill that may be demonstrated above or below age-expectation levels during an evaluation.

6. Perseveration

Perseveration is like a broken record; it involves doing the same thing over and over again. Perseveration can be evidenced verbally (e.g., the child who continues repeating the same phrase incessantly) or physically (e.g., the child who plays with the same toy in the same place in the same way for hours or until interrupted). Perseveration is also evidenced through acute fascination with specific objects or movements, such as flushing a toilet or watching a circling ceiling fan. Perseveration for verbal routines, questions, and directions also occurs with high frequency among children with autism.

7. Echolalia

Echolalia is a primary characteristic of communication in children with autism. *Echolalia*, from the word *echo*, means repeating exactly what was heard. Echolalia can be immediate, like a parrot that quickly echoes what it heard, or delayed. Delayed echolalia means that the echoed segment doesn't occur for minutes, hours, days, weeks, months, or years after the initial input. Many children with autism indiscriminately echo what they have heard. I have often heard what I sounded like as a teacher through the mouths of children who were echolalic!

Echolalia was misunderstood for many years. For a time, extinguishing echolalia was advocated as a means to achieve meaningful speech. Experience with autism over the years has helped professionals understand that it is not a matter of extinguishing verbal echoes, but shaping them to be used meaningfully.

For example, perhaps you've greeted someone by saying "How are you?" I'd venture that almost every person reading this book has repeated that phrase recently. So you all engaged in echolalia! "How are you?" is not an original, creative utterance; it has been generated before. The key is knowing when to use a phrase to communicate effectively. Chapter 5, Communication Intervention, addresses shaping echolalia toward meaningful speech.

8. Identity Concept

Discrimination of identity can be extremely difficult and puzzling within the syndrome of autism. It is common for a child with autism not to respond to his name or recognize it in print with any sense of ownership. Temple Grandin discussed the difficulty she had in knowing where she stopped and an object started, such as her hand in contact with a chair (*Thinking in Pictures*, 1995).

Relating to other people and themselves also plays a part in the development of identity for children with autism. One small child fell on the playground at recess. He ran to the teacher and calmly stated, "You fell and hurt your knee. Go and get a Band-Aid®," when it was the child himself who was actually hurt.

Pronouns are particularly confusing for individuals with autism. They often refer to themselves by their proper names rather than *me* or *I*. The use of first-person pronouns is almost completely absent prior to intervention. Characteristics to note during observation include confusion with use of *I, you, me, us, we* pronouns and a tendency to always use proper names rather than pronouns.

Pronouns discriminating gender can also be problematic; gender is an abstract concept which requires time for the child with autism to understand. *He/she, Mr./Mrs., Daddy/Mommy* are often reversed or used incorrectly. Generalization can also occur; if the first teacher ever introduced was a *Mrs.*, any teacher's name is prefaced with *Mrs.* One of my college clients assumed all teachers at the college level were *Dr.* He gradually learned this was not the case, but couldn't drop the polite title that translated as college teacher; instead, he added a second title to differentiate. So a college instructor who did not have a doctoral degree might be referred to as *Mr. Dr. Smith*. The system worked fine until he encountered a husband and wife team of professors who both had doctoral degrees. It was much too ambiguous for his comfort to refer to them both as *Dr. Marlow*. His solution was to add second titles for them following the title — *Dr. Mr. Marlow* and *Dr. Mrs. Marlow*.

9. Ritualism

The need for ordered routine is a dominant characteristic in autism. Some children are ritualistic to the point of demonstrating obsessive-compulsive tendencies. Ritualism can be observed in children's verbal routines as well as nonverbal behaviors.

One ritualistic characteristic that parents and teachers often note is a child's necessity to impose a sense of order, usually by lining items up in a row, such as blocks, crayons, puzzle pieces, or other items. One preschool child very meticulously took all the carefully-grouped chairs for a neighborhood gathering and lined them up in a straight row down the middle of the street!

Teachers frequently note that children with autism have difficulty dealing with a change in schedule. The routine of the school day becomes almost sacred to many of these children. Modifications can create great anxiety, followed by behavioral outbursts. Parents and teachers also tell stories of problems encountered when furniture or room decorations are changed or are out of place. The child with autism will either attempt to return any item out of place or become very upset that the routine has been altered visually and physically.

Verbal routines are also observed easily in a school setting. Verbal children with autism often anticipate or lip synch directions for expected activities. Sometimes they request that a teacher say a particular phrase for them. Verbal routines and question routines can also be used as a calming technique. For example, in the film *Rainman*, Dustin Hoffman's autistic character would recite "Who's on first," an Abbott and Costello routine, when becoming anxious or overstimulated.

Despite the problems of coping with ritualistic behaviors, some of these same characteristics can facilitate intervention. Using routines can work well to increase tolerance for the external world and disruptive stimuli. The use of routines for intervention will be addressed in later chapters.

10. Mental Rigidity

Mechanical learning of symbolic code systems which maintain a constant value is often a splinter strength within individuals with autism. The ability to complete mathematical calculations very rapidly without using paper, a pencil, or a calculator is well substantiated in the autism literature. Many children with autism are proficient phonetic decoders and can "read" simple words very early. The glitch occurs in comprehension of the code system; that's when mental rigidity becomes apparent.

In the film *Rainman*, Dustin Hoffman portrayed an autistic adult who had incredible numeric calculation ability, but no concept of the functional value of money. There are articles and books about people with autism who can reproduce music or art, but who cannot create original works of art or music. One client, for example, could "read" the first consonant and vowel in any word, but couldn't point to the picture of the word she read.

Mental rigidity is cracking a code without understanding what the decoded information means or what to do with it. The challenge for teachers and parents is to help the child fill in meaning, adding comprehension to empty code-breaking skills.

11. Attention Deficit

Individuals with autism are frequently misdiagnosed as having attention deficit problems. While attention span can be very short for directed activities, it is important to evaluate sustained attention for activities of the child's choosing. For example, if a child with autism can sit for hours working the same puzzles over and over again, then there probably is not an attention deficit disorder. With autism, a biochemical wall may interfere with stimuli and prevent it from being received or processed by the child. Certain stimuli may be aversive, overwhelming, or anxiety provoking. The resulting behaviors may parallel attention deficit disorder, but have a very different cause. The poor attention in autism may not be due to an inability to discriminate and attend to relevant stimuli, but rather an inability to receive or respond to stimuli. Neurological differences between attention deficit disorder and autism are also addressed in subsequent chapters.

Attention deficit disorder can co-occur within autism as one component of the syndrome, but the informal data must be analyzed very carefully. Observational data should balance examples of attention across both externally and internally chosen activities for the child being evaluated.

12. Impaired Social Interaction

Significant impairment in social interaction is one of the major criteria for autism. The poor interaction usually goes across three planes: relating to self, relating to others, and relating to the environment.

Poor identity concept and relating to oneself has been discussed previously in this section. Using a proper name when referring to oneself, poor recognition of one's body in space, and a lack of emotional response are examples of behaviors which indicate an inability to relate to self. Difficulty relating to other people can usually be observed in:

- poor eye contact

- little or no interactive play with other children

- a lack of response to verbal questions or nonverbal actions

- limited response to activities of other individuals

A poor relationship with the environment generates safety concerns for children with autism. A child may not understand dangerous consequences in the environment, such as touching a hot stove, walking in front of a car, or letting go while swinging. An inability to process and respond appropriately to environmental stimuli is usually readily apparent during informal observation.

13. Mechanical Movement and/or Speech

The individual with autism may appear almost robot-like in motor movement and speech patterns. An artificial appearance during interaction can be observed readily within a classroom or home setting.

Communication is often marked by problems in suprasegmentals of speech production (e.g., pitch, rate, inflection, or prosody). Rate can be very rapid, compromising intelligibility and making verbalizations sound like jargon, or very slow and measured. Inflectional variation can be minimal, resulting in a flat, monotone vocal production that seems void of sincerity and emotion.

Limb movement can be stiff and uncoordinated, resulting in some unusual gaits. General posture can also be stilted, awkward, and noticeably different.

14. Perimeter Walking

A peculiar path for walking or circling a room is often noted by teachers and parents. Children with autism tend to walk the edge of a defined space. Some children will venture into an area, but when they become overwhelmed, they plaster themselves against a wall or rub up against the outer boundaries of the room. One preschool child routinely walked the perimeter of the room, playground, or hallway. While on a field trip to a farm, he was momentarily "misplaced." He was found, to the great relief of his teachers, walking the outer edges of a corn field!

Perimeter walking behavior might appear rather bizarre to most people, but actually has a fairly simple explanation once you understand the components of autism. Activity and interaction usually occur in the center of a room. The inner space of an area can be very threatening to an individual with autism because expectations for compliance and interaction increase within that space. The outer perimeter of a room is much safer and calming for a child with autism. Activity is more limited on the outer edges and fewer people wander there, decreasing the chances that the child will have to interact.

Sample Observation Reports

Summarizing observational data to substantiate a diagnosis of autism requires experience, but this task is less intimidating when you know which behavioral components to focus upon. Descriptive data is critical in supporting or refuting the diagnostic criterion for the disability. The syndrome nature of autism further necessitates accurate behavioral impressions.

Two sample reports are provided from my case files in Appendix 3A and Appendix 3B, pages 46-51. Names have been deleted and data has been rearranged to disguise specific clients. The format for presenting observational information in a diagnostic summary report, however, remains intact. Both reports are observation evaluations of children. The first evaluation resulted in a diagnosis of autism and observational data was incorporated to substantiate the label. The second remained at a label of pervasive developmental disorder with reasons stated, as well as suggestions for future prognosis.

Identification information, referral reasons, and pertinent background information are summarized first in the reports. The Observation Impressions section reviews the client's behavioral characteristics. Each paragraph addresses observations in a specific area, such as communication, motor, social interaction, and academics.

The Conclusion section attempts to substantiate the diagnostic conclusion drawn from the observational evaluation. Specific characteristics are added to clarify impressions, or deleted so that the bigger picture is not lost in specific details.

The Recommendations section is very important. In many cases, the teachers and/or parents are aware of a disability, but especially want to know how to program to meet the child's needs and modify the presenting behaviors. Make recommendations as specific as possible to the child's present setting so that clinical implementation of ideas suggested can begin expediently.

Summary Comments

➡ The criteria for diagnosing autism is primarily descriptive behavior, resulting in the need for accurate and careful observational data to substantiate a diagnosis.

➡ Experience and knowledge of pertinent characteristics within the behavioral profile for autism are critical for accurate evaluation and diagnoses.

➡ There are observational rating scales that include key behavioral components and enable you to compile data into composite skill areas. One example is the *Gilliam Autism Rating Scale* (1995), the cover sheet of which is included in Appendix 3C, page 52. Observational data is summarized into four major areas: stereotyped behaviors, communication, social interaction, and general development. The composite scores yield an autism quotient that can be interpreted into the probability of the presence of autism.

➡ Informal observational data can also be summarized into major skill areas.

➡ Observation evaluation reports addressing a variety of skills should call attention to a combination of both strengths and weaknesses in the analysis.

45

Appendix 3A: Example Observation Report

Name: Maurice G.   Age: 9 years, 2 months   Date: 1/xx/96
Site: XX Elementary School   Evaluator: Gail J. Richard, Ph.D., CCC/SLP

Informal Observation Impressions

Maurice was observed at XX Elementary School in XX at the request of school personnel and with permission of his parents. Concerns prompting the evaluation focused on educational programming strategies to enhance learning and minimize behavioral characteristics present. Although trainable mentally handicapped (TMH) was listed as the primary disability on the IEP with a secondary disability of speech-language, materials from school personnel submitted prior to the evaluation suggested autism as the primary disability.

Maurice frequently wandered around the classroom. His eye contact was poor. Maurice exhibited self-stimulatory behaviors and was unresponsive to peer interaction. He did not complete tasks independently or focus without adult attention. He appeared to accomplish most tasks through rote repetition of demonstrated movements rather than with meaningful understanding. Maurice showed fine-motor delays when printing on the board, but did recognize the alphabet letters and wrote them on command within words. His independent typing was fairly efficient and accurate for simple words presented visually.

Maurice was primarily nonverbal and used no intelligible speech. He made self-stimulatory vocal sounds as well as squeals and screams when frustrated. His verbal productions consisted primarily of an initial bilabial or velar stop-plosive consonant with a vowel. Sign language was used effectively as a focusing technique and Maurice responded appropriately to several simple signs, such as *sit* and *stand*. He did not initiate any signing to the teachers, but did imitate some signs upon demand.

Self-stimulatory movements observed included frequent mouthing of materials, finger stimulation repetitively on his lips, head patting, rocking, and tactile rubbing of materials. These behaviors suggested a neurological need for sensory integration of an intense physical nature that is not currently being met. A compulsive need for routine/order was also noted. Maurice moved through the building very proficiently to various locations required within his daily schedule.

Conclusions

Maurice demonstrated a behavioral profile consistent with a diagnosis of autism. The four primary characteristics are described below, followed by observations which substantiate their presence in his learning profile.

1. Qualitative impairment in social interaction

    Maurice did not initiate or respond to peers within the classroom. Spontaneous interactions were not observed and adult interactions prompted by Maurice were to meet his immediate needs. He appeared to be in his own world much of the time, and was not responsive to stimuli presented in the environment or by other people unless focus was ensured by an adult.

2. Qualitative impairment in communication

    Maurice demonstrated communication deficits, including difficulty with the ability to process/attach meaning to auditory stimuli, minimal expressive verbalization, and very poor awareness of communication demands (e.g., lack of eye contact and turn taking).

3. Restrictive repetitive and stereotyped patterns of behavior, interests, and activities

   Maurice demonstrated the need for routines and compulsive order in his world. Self-stimulatory behaviors and motor differences were also observed.

4. Delays or abnormal functioning with onset prior to age three

   Case history information suggests that the disability has been present from early childhood, with documentation supporting an early onset of atypical characteristics affecting the broad spectrum of development.

Recommendations

Maurice's school placement appeared to be appropriate at the present time, but modifications to increase productive use of his focus in the classroom setting should be implemented. The special education classroom with a small student-teacher ratio is definitely beneficial to maximize Maurice's learning potential. Benefits of the regular education setting appeared to be minimal at this point, but the students were receptive to Maurice, interacted with him, and he was not disruptive during the time I observed. Suggested specific areas for educational programming are the following:

I. Emphasize speech-language development to increase meaningful communication interactions within the educational setting.

   A. Initiate pragmatic interactive communication behaviors. Teach Maurice ways to initiate or respond to interaction with peers through very concrete examples and visual models. Teach the use of polite routines (e.g., *please* and *thank you*) in specific situations that occur frequently throughout the school day.

   B. Maurice's receptive comprehension of language was questionable. Encourage Maurice's awareness of language meaning by pairing visual and verbal stimuli in classroom lessons. Once his comprehension has become more consistent, occasionally withhold the visual and/or verbal stimulus to encourage him to attach meaning to information presented in the classroom. Use questions consistently to check Maurice's accurate processing of the information that he reads or types.

   C. Explore an expressive or reliable output system. At present, Maurice does a variety of things, including verbalizing, typing, and signing. However, meaningfulness within any of the methodologies is questionable. Encourage more independent typing or picture pointing and evaluate these systems for meaningfulness and consistency. Motivating reinforcements may increase Maurice's desire to participate in activities.

   D. Shape verbal productions through oral-motor exercises (e.g., blowing bubbles, party favors, or kazoos) and automatic speech (e.g., rhymes and songs). Introduce "power words" that, when produced, have an immediate, positive impact on Maurice's ability to control his environment (e.g., *eat* or *potty*).

   E. Sign language worked well to focus and regulate Maurice visually, and should continue to be used for these purposes.

II. Incorporate sensory integration into educational programming as part of Maurice's everyday schedule to facilitate better focused attention within the classroom.

   A. An evaluation by a physical/occupational therapist to evaluate Maurice's sensory system should be completed. This evaluation can assist school personnel and parents in incorporating sensory integration into Maurice's daily activities.

B. Schedule sensory integration on a regular basis to allow down time between academic demands. Structure and time physical exercise or release to allow Maurice to understand how to request down time in a more age-appropriate manner. Productive time might be facilitated by having adults provide sensory integration (e.g., rubbing Maurice's back), freeing his energy for academic focus and task comprehension.

C. Shape or modify inappropriate behaviors by providing replacement sensory stimulation items. For example, oral stimulation might be more hygienic using a mouth guard or block. Tactile hand stimulation might replace finger flicking of his lips by using a Koosh® or squeeze ball. Desensitization to various foods' taste, smell, and texture can be accomplished through requiring a brief exposure, but not actual consumption.

III. Establish academic limits and structure to increase Maurice's compliant, focused behavior.

A. Try using a visual timer to structure work and down time concretely. At present, Maurice manipulates and resists adults who are in control of how long he works or when he gets breaks. An external objective stimulus may improve his focused attention.

B. Introduce concrete, functional academic tasks. Using real objects will facilitate a more meaningful interaction for Maurice. Cause-effect and activities which have closure will be less anxiety provoking and more meaningful to Maurice. A very clear purpose and opportunity for visual demonstration and motor involvement will facilitate Maurice's participation. Functional jobs to build independence can also be tried.

C. Introduce tasks through a task analysis approach with clearly delineated steps when possible. Use routines or numbered steps to help Maurice learn the order, decrease anxiety, and make closure concrete. Pair pictures with print while exploring this option to work toward more independence on Maurice's part in completing activities.

D. Structure academic tasks to include visual-motor techniques to maximize Maurice's ability to understand the task and increase attention toward completion. Be aware of his compulsive tendency toward imposing order rather than understanding your directions.

E. Be cautious of overtalking. Maurice tuned out auditory stimuli which was overwhelming or too complex for him to process. Simplify to telegraphic speech, using only pertinent words and signs. Punctuate or emphasize auditory signals you want Maurice to focus on by preceding them with silence.

Thank you for the opportunity to interact with Maurice's teachers and parents. It is recommended that current placement continue with implementation and exploration of some of the techniques listed above and discussed in the conference at the conclusion of my visit. If I can be of further assistance, please contact me.

Appendix 3B: Example Observation Report

Name: __David R.__   Age: __5 years__   Date: __1/xx/96__
Site: __Early Childhood Program__   Evaluator: __Gail J. Richard, Ph.D., CCC/SLP__

Informal Observation Impressions

David was observed at the request of school personnel and with permission of his parents. Concerns prompting the evaluation were in regard to the primary disability contributing to David's developmental delays, and subsequent suggestions for educational programming to best meet his needs. The observation occurred in his early childhood classroom on a typical day.

David was an attractive little boy who was involved in group books and songs when the observer entered the classroom. He sat compliantly and participated in group singing. David had obviously memorized the books; he could recite along with the teacher as they were read and easily predict what would come on subsequent pages. His motor participation in the songs was delayed and awkward as compared to other children in the classroom. David was also observed to be easily overstimulated, and reacted perseveratively in an exaggerated manner to pleasurable stimuli, such as knocking over blocks after stacking them.

David demonstrated appropriate play, but he seemed to prefer isolated play rather than interactive. However, when other children joined him, he did not become upset or resistant and appeared to enjoy participating with them in a limited way. David was intensely aware of the adults in the room and watched them carefully. He was echolalic in response to teacher questions, but he did respond appropriately physically when prompted with visual cues. David was extremely dependent on the teacher's nonverbal gestural cues. He also seemed very dependent on routines; tantrums or resistant behaviors were triggered when an activity was nearing completion.

David maintained focus fairly well once he understood the task or expectation. His alphabet, shape, and number recognition were very good. David's motor skills were poor, but he accepted help readily from an adult. Motor movement overflow was noted during fine-motor tasks, such as tongue protrusion and movement while cutting. His verbal jargon appeared to be a calming, self-stimulatory behavior.

Conclusions

David demonstrated behaviors consistent with a pervasive developmental disorder. His neurological immaturity and differences were evidenced by self-stimulatory behaviors, motor deficits, and speech-language deficits (e.g., echolalia and jargon). David's sensory system differences were evidenced by a hypersensitive response to taste and texture of foods. Self-stimulatory responses noted included perseverative laughing, jargon verbalizations, and some hand movements. While reciprocal social interaction was delayed, David was very aware of his environment and other people. Behavioral resistance was usually in direct response to verbal directions or a change in routine. The behavioral profile evidenced does not indicate autism, but neurological immaturity and withdrawal has resulted in many of the characteristics being present in a mild form. These characteristics should continue to diminish with focused programming to stimulate neurological development while building David's confidence through positive language interaction experiences.

Residual affects of this developmental delay can include:

1. an oral-motor delay, resulting in difficulty acquiring voluntary speech-production abilities.

2. a language processing-based learning disability, resulting in difficulty attaching meaning to information presented through the auditory modality. This results in increased visual awareness to compensate through another sensory modality.

3. a pragmatic language deficit, resulting from avoidance of interaction and isolation from peers during socialization opportunities.

Future evaluations should focus on identifying residual problems, such as motor deficits, language processing/learning disability, or pragmatic language deficits. The immediate educational programming goals should be to compensate for the immature neurological development, but encourage and reinforce opportunities for programming and output in these areas.

Recommendations

David is presently using his strengths to avoid his weaknesses. For example, he used visual examples to complete tasks independently rather than initiate verbal interactions for assistance. He also resisted auditory-only stimuli because it was so difficult to process, and relied on visual stimuli for learning. His neurological delays will require stimulation and focus to develop and mature. Therefore, it is important to continue stimulating his deficit sensory systems, and to encourage David to program and coordinate his responses neurologically.

A. Speech and language therapy should address the receptive processing and expressive output deficits evidenced. David was aware of and frustrated by his difficulty attaching meaning to verbal stimulation. Many of his resistant behaviors appeared to be triggered by anxiety in response to verbal directions and comments.

1. Continue to stimulate speech/language production, but with simplified expressive expectations. Structure verbal output to approximate short phrases rather than complex sentences. David might experience more success if attempting to program and produce shorter verbal units. Also, accept and reinforce any verbalization he produces, even if it is unintelligible. An imprecise verbalization indicates a voluntary attempt on David's part to produce a meaningful response rather than echoed output.

2. Stimulate David's oral-motor coordination by using visual reinforcements as motivation (e.g., party favors, horns, bubbles, or candles to encourage a sustained, voluntary air flow). A kazoo could be used for sustained voiced air flow. Animal noises and nonsense noises can also be stimulated. David's oral-motor coordination may be facilitated by general motor movement overflow, such as jumping up and down saying "pop" or crawling on the floor while producing "s."

3. Songs, poems, finger plays, and memorization can also be effective for stimulating voluntary speech. The pre-programmed sequences reduce the coordination stress for rate/rhythm and word choice, allowing David to experience success in speech production with a reduced neurological demand.

4. Encourage and manipulate peer interactions in non-threatening and low-verbal-output situations. David avoids interaction due to his awareness of deficiencies in his ability to carry the load in verbal interaction. This behavior could result in later pragmatic deficits from lack of experience with social language use. Use routines for consistent pragmatic language prompts to increase David's confidence during reciprocal social interaction.

5. Encourage David's language processing development. He is struggling to attach meaning to auditory stimulation. Simplify language models and present concrete objects with the auditory models. Gradually fade the visual cues to promote language processing.

B. Classroom programming should build on David's strengths and comfort tasks to promote confidence and development of weak areas.

1. David is very comfortable with concrete objective academics, such as alphabet recognition, numbers, and shapes. Use these concepts to increase processing in the classroom. For example, building word recognition skills may be a concrete task that David will enjoy while enhancing opportunities for language processing with the visual/graphic cues.

2. The computer may be an excellent learning tool for David. The anxiety of verbal stimuli would be reduced, visual stimulation would be constant, and the combination could increase his attention for focused learning.

3. Manipulate learning opportunities that encourage David to use his auditory channel as a primary stimulus modality, with visual or tactile as a secondary modality. Examples might include cassette tapes with worksheets, taped stories which David can follow along visually, scavenger hunts, or playing detective. The activity's continuation should be based on careful listening, but supplemented with visual or tactile cues and reinforcements.

4. Use multiple-modality teaching to alleviate frustration and compensate for a neurologically immature system. David will benefit from experiential teaching introduced through many simultaneous sensory modalities (e.g., visual, tactile, auditory, olfactory, and taste).

5. Use cues, prompts, and gestures to assist processing information, particularly attaching auditory meaning.

C. An occupational therapy evaluation would be beneficial to evaluate David's motor development and neurological sensory sensitivity. Suggestions for stimulation to promote neurological development in the classroom and at home would be beneficial.

I appreciated the opportunity to observe David and talk with his parents and school staff. Definite improvements have resulted from the educational programming currently and should continue with the refinements discussed in the conference. I anticipate David's continued progress in the future and I believe David will enjoy the challenge of learning. If I can be of further assistance, please contact me.

GARS

Gilliam Autism Rating Scale

SUMMARY/RESPONSE FORM

Section I. Identifying Information

Subject's Name _____

Address _____

_____

Parents'/Guardians' Names _____

School _____

Examiner's Name _____

Examiner's Title _____

Date of GARS Rating _____ _____
Year Month

Subject's Date of Birth _____ _____
Year Month

Subject's Age _____ _____
Year Month

Section II. Score Summary

Subtests	Raw Score	SS	%ile	SE$_M$
Stereotyped Behaviors	___	___	___	1
Communication	___	___	___	1
Social Interaction	___	___	___	1
Developmental	___	___	___	1
Sum of Standard Scores				
Autism Quotient		___	___	3

Section III. Interpretation Guide

Subtest Standard Scores	Autism Quotient	Degree of Severity	Probability of Autism
		High	
17–19	131+	↑	Very High
15–16	121–130		High
13–14	111–120		Above Average
8–12	90–110		Average
6–7	80–89		Below Average
4–5	70–79	↓	Low
1–3	≤69		Very Low
		Low	

Section IV. Profile of Scores

GARS Subtests

Other Measures of Intelligence, Achievement, or Adaptive Behavior

Standard Scores	Stereotyped Behaviors	Communication	Social Interaction	Developmental	Autism Quotient	Other Quotients	Test Used	Test Used	Test Used	Test Used
					•	160	•	•	•	•
					•	155	•	•	•	•
20	•	•	•	•	•	150	•	•	•	•
19	•	•	•	•	•	145	•	•	•	•
18	•	•	•	•		140	•	•	•	•
17	•	•	•	•		135	•	•	•	•
16	•	•	•	•	•	130	•	•	•	•
15	•	•	•	•		125	•	•	•	•
14	•	•	•	•	•	120	•	•	•	•
13	•	•	•	•		115	•	•	•	•
12	•	•	•	•	•	110	•	•	•	•
11	•	•	•	•		105	•	•	•	•
10	•	•	•	•	•	100	•	•	•	•
9	•	•	•	•		95	•	•	•	•
8	•	•	•	•		90	•	•	•	•
7	•	•	•	•	•	85	•	•	•	•
6	•	•	•	•		80	•	•	•	•
5	•	•	•	•		75	•	•	•	•
4	•	•	•	•	•	70	•	•	•	•
3	•	•	•	•	•	65	•	•	•	•
2	•	•	•	•	•	60	•	•	•	•
1	•	•	•	•	•	55	•	•	•	•

Additional copies of this form (#6822) are available from PRO-ED, 8700 Shoal Creek Blvd., Austin, TX 78757, 512/451-3246.

Reprinted by permission from Pro Ed, Austin, TX 512/451-3246

Chapter 4
Team Coordination and Responsibilities

The 'dis' in 'disability' seemed written in letters ten feet tall;
it cast a shadow over the fact there was any ability at all to be
found in that word.

Donna Williams
Somebody Somewhere

Team Philosophy

The syndrome of autism is represented by many different characteristics. Meeting the needs of individuals with autism requires coordinated effort among professionals and parents on the team. Information from a variety of specialists is critical to determine techniques for modifying characteristics within the syndrome, thus allowing all children with autism to achieve their full potential.

Autism has moved from the domain of being an exclusive medical diagnosis. It is now an acceptable educational label that can be determined by a multidisciplinary team within the school setting. However, the diagnostic label of autism does not in itself lead to effective programming by individuals interacting with the student. Professionals across a variety of disciplines need to discriminate the primary components of each individual collaboratively, and then understand how all the pieces within the syndrome fit together.

One critical aspect of team intervention is to maintain focus on the whole child. While each individual discipline may evaluate a specific area of symptoms, all the pieces must be re-assembled to form the complete picture of the individual child with autism. Often the perspective is lost while a particular professional looks through the specific microscope of her specialization. The team must remember to weigh the syndrome pieces against each other equitably.

It is also important to focus carefully on the abilities of an individual with autism. Professional evaluation often results in a list of "can't do's," a delineation of deficits or problems. A responsible team balances deficits with abilities, delineating strengths and areas where there are no problems.

To use the analogy from earlier chapters, the team must determine the pieces of each individual's autism puzzle. Programming decisions and intervention effectiveness will correlate directly with the accuracy of the team's evaluation results. Diverse and comprehensive feedback from a team of professionals should facilitate more effective intervention.

Team Decisions

A number of primary and secondary decisions must be made by the multidisciplinary team. Therefore, the team must function well as a unit with a common philosophy and respect across disciplines. It is not uncommon for one team member to be more dominant in a leadership capacity. Even as a leader, however, that person must utilize and respect the input from each professional on the team, including the parents. Each team member should share impressions and data with the other professionals and parents in the meeting. The composite summary of information can then lead to solid programming decisions.

A parent attending one of my presentations shared a story emphasizing the importance of weighing each team member's input appropriately. Two of her children had disabilities, so she had attended many staffings over the years. She was frustrated by dominant professionals who had had minimal contact with her children, yet whose decisions prevailed in staffings. One of her children's autistic behavior in evaluation situations with strangers masked a great deal of ability. She had great confidence in the child's teacher, but both teacher and parent impressions were usually overruled in multidisciplinary staffings.

This mother related that her fantasy was to take in school pictures of three children from a classroom, including her own child. She would then place the pictures on the table and ask each professional to point to her child's photograph. All those who couldn't identify the student for whom the staffing was being held must leave! It was her opinion that if they couldn't even identify her child, then they hadn't spent enough time with the child to be involved in critical educational decisions. Something to think about!

Major decisions team members need to address are listed below, followed by discussion.

Team Decisions

1. Primary disability diagnosis
2. Deficits and needs of the individual
3. Professional services required
4. Educational goals
5. Educational placement

1. Primary Disability Diagnosis

The first decision is to determine the primary disability. Feedback from a variety of individuals usually assists in making a differential diagnosis. The nature of developmental disabilities necessitates diagnosis based on observation. Including multiple perspectives facilitates a more confident decision process for a team. The group can then delineate collectively the symptoms that substantiate the autism syndrome.

Differential diagnosis within the spectrum of PDD is a challenging task. The experience team members have in working with developmental disabilities can significantly affect the group's comfort level in determining the primary disability. Chapter 2, Diagnosis of Autism, addresses some of the critical features to keep in mind when attempting to discriminate the primary disability.

The Federal definition of autism is part of the *Individuals with Disabilities Education Act (IDEA)*. Autism is, therefore, a primary disability for the educational setting. Many states have already implemented their own criteria for diagnosing autism. Whether an educational or a medical approach is taken, the multidisciplinary team should substantiate diagnosis consistent with the criteria designated within a particular setting.

2. Deficits and Needs of the Individual

A second group responsibility is to determine the unique needs of the individual with autism. The symptomatic profile of strengths and weaknesses should be compiled, based on the evaluations and disciplines represented. At this point in the process, a child's needs should not be deleted from the list just because services may not be available. The purpose of this step is to reach agreement on the pieces which add up to the individual's puzzle of autism. Chapter 3 identifies some of these possible pieces.

A complete determination of needs may require outside or independent evaluations for team consideration. For example, not all educational settings have an occupational or physical therapist on staff, yet an assessment of motor development and sensory system responsiveness is an important piece in the autism puzzle.

3. Professional Services Required

Once agreement has been reached on the aspects that need to be addressed, determination of professional services and degree of involvement must be examined. This phase of teamwork can become problematic as philosophical differences become apparent. A parent or professional must carefully evaluate desired services vs. needed services.

While a utopian environment might be desirable, the team and the parents must maintain a realistic outlook. The school setting is not charged to maximize services; its responsibility is to meet needs. There are always attractive options available that may carry a high price tag. The team must decide objectively which services are critical to a child's progress. Luxury services may be available for children with autism, but if our budget doesn't allow luxury items, we make do with functional services. The comparison to our own personal finances as we weigh dreams vs. necessities is a good analogy. A professional or parent may decide to provide a luxury service independently; it does not have to be provided by an educational setting simply because it is available or desired.

The other end of the continuum is when services are obviously needed, but not being provided at an appropriate level to impact a child's development. Professionals must ethically evaluate the type, amount, and service delivery models agreed upon in multidisciplinary staffings. Personal agendas or concerns should not compromise services provided to meet needs.

The team should generate and consider compromises when decisions on services cannot be resolved easily. An administrator may object to occupational therapy due to cost; other team members may feel the fine-motor deficits necessitate the services. A possible resolution might be to offer consultative occupational therapy services to develop and monitor goals that existing staff members implement. Another option might be using an occupational therapy aide on a regular basis, supervised and monitored by a certified therapist. Creative options abound when teams avoid ultimatums and focus on shared intentions rather than differences.

4. Educational Goals

Deficits which need to be addressed for the individual with autism are addressed by goals. Goal statements should be measurable, objective behaviors the child will demonstrate. Methods and specific techniques the professional might use are not appropriate for goal statements. Goals pertain to the child's progress and how it will be evaluated.

An educational program must have objectives that are integrated across disciplines. Autism does not respond well to services that are provided separately and distinctly. It is difficult to accomplish generalization when services are compartmentalized. Consistency among service providers and all settings results in greater progress.

The concept of integrated services may require some re-thinking within the educational setting. I have attended many staffings in which each professional reviewed individual goals. Then, an administrator collected all the papers and stapled them together as though integration had been achieved.

True integration of goals is driven by the individual's needs as defined by the team. An identified deficit is then addressed by specific goals to remediate the weak area. Anyone who intervenes on that specific deficit is then an implementor who is involved in remediating that need. For example, communication goals should not be the exclusive domain of the speech-language pathologist. Everything a teacher does is couched in language. Sometimes the best focus for language is facilitated during spinning and deep-pressure exercises in physical therapy. All team members need to work together in implementing goals with a shared responsibility across disciplines. Areas to include in an informal diagnostic profile are listed below.

Informal Diagnostic Profile Areas	
Social Interaction	relating to self, others, and the environment
Communication	verbal and nonverbal receptive and expressive
Motor	self-stimulatory differences gross- and fine-motor development sensory system differences
Behavior	adaptive and maladaptive
Academics	specific academic skill development
Cognitive	cognitive functioning level

Write objectives to address these areas, not to address the disciplines represented on the team. The role of various professionals in implementing the objectives should be apparent from the wording of the goals. Overlap is essential for generalization across environments. Appendices 4A and 4B, pages 64-66, offer a hypothetical case profile of a five-year-old boy making the transition from early childhood programming to kindergarten. Example goal statements to address needs follow in Appendix 4C, page 67.

5. Educational Placement

The team's decisions are then used to determine the educational setting in which the goals can be implemented and services provided most effectively. Placement decisions can become controversial and are another aspect of teaming that can be jeopardized without mutual respect among team members.

Because autism is a syndrome disorder, any one aspect should not be used exclusively to determine placement. For example, with mental impairments, the IQ usually determines the level of classroom placement. However, with autism, IQ is rarely a reliable assessment of cognitive ability during the early school years. Psychological evaluation entails a significant language component, one of the major deficits in autism, and involves relating to an individual, a second major deficit in autism. Placement decisions relying solely on IQ test results could be faulty.

Furthermore, a diagnosis of autism should not result in an autism classroom. In the late 1970s as the educational system adjusted to federal special education laws, there was a misconception that a label equaled a classroom. For example, if a district labeled children learning disabled, then a learning-disabilities classroom had to be created. While common features exist within autism, a classroom of children with the disability would probably result in chaos for everyone, including the teacher and students!

A second problem concerns the continuum of severity within autism. Key characteristics range from very mild to very severe. Simply reaching consensus on a diagnosis of autism does not result in a specific logical placement. The pieces of the individual's profile must be examined individually to determine placement options. Chapter 3 includes some general suggestions using prognostic factors of communication and IQ in discussion of the Quadrant Theory (pages 24-27). The multidisciplinary team must consider all options when determining placement for individuals with autism. Primary factors to consider for placement decisions are listed below, followed by discussion.

Primary Placement Factors	
Chronological Age	Curriculum Types
Behavior	Support Services
Language Level	Student-Teacher Ratio
Cognitive/Intellectual Level	

Chronological Age

I am frequently amazed to discover children six and seven years old who are placed in early childhood classrooms on a rules-exception status. The rationale generally relates to team fear or confusion about placement in the larger system. The transition to a more age-appropriate setting may provoke anxiety, but it's a necessary step. Delaying the inevitable doesn't justify avoiding a placement change. Peer models, interaction, and motivation for involvement in school activities are not enhanced by maintaining a preschool environment.

Behavior

Behavior can be a frustrating factor within autism. Professionals tend to focus on behavioral problems, since these characteristics interfere with learning. Discriminating maladaptive behaviors is important in identifying needs and generating goals for a child with autism. However, it should not become the primary focus for placement decisions.

The issue of behavior must be balanced. Professionals and parents are usually accurate in listing maladaptive behaviors that are a concern for educational programming. If a child's placement is based on maladaptive behaviors, however, the frequency of maladaptive behaviors is likely to increase! A list of adaptive behaviors must also be introduced — the situations or people with whom the child shows compliant, focused behavior. If the placement can maximize controlled behavior times and minimize disruptive behavior situations, then programming may be more successful. Specific strategies for dealing with behavioral components of the autistic syndrome are addressed in detail in Chapter 7.

Language Level

Language within the syndrome of autism can be very misleading. The expressive echolalia often misrepresents receptive comprehension. A child may echo language heard within the environment without understanding or processing what was said. Therefore, it is important to evaluate the child's expressive language carefully.

In general, receptive understanding of language is assumed in expressive output. When people speak on a topic, we presume they understand the content. This comprehension cannot be presumed in individuals with autism who exhibit verbal echolalia and perseveration. Receptive and expressive language levels must be evaluated separately.

Cognitive/Intellectual Level

Research literature suggests mental impairment in at least 70% of individuals with autism. The intellectual ability of an individual with autism must be consistent with educational expectations. An accurate evaluation of IQ through standardized tests may not be accomplished until approximately age 10. However, teams can use behavioral observation of functional levels, interests, and aptitudes to determine an appropriate placement.

Curriculum Types

Since educational curriculum models vary with placement options, a team must consider if a functional, applied, vocational curriculum is more appropriate than a more abstract, academic curriculum. The presentation style and expected pace of learning also vary within curriculums. An educable mentally-impaired classroom vs. a trainable mentally-impaired classroom may have vastly different curriculums, even though the child with autism may qualify for either due to difficulty accurately assessing IQ. A regular classroom may be the most appropriate school setting, but also require modification, such as an aide, resource room, or supplemental services.

Support Services

A student transitioning from early childhood to kindergarten may have several placement options. The availability of resource professionals may become an important consideration in the decision. For example, school A might have a speech-language pathologist every day, while school B has services twice a week. The placement choice should maximize support services needed early in the child's education, with potential to gradually reduce over time.

Student-Teacher Ratio

The number of students in a classroom can impact a child with autism dramatically. The noise level increases proportionately and can trigger disruptive behavior as the child attempts to cope with sensory input. A teacher's ability to be flexible and generate modifications as needed also decreases with more students to consider. Special education classrooms often have a smaller ratio of teachers and aides to students. Until a child has adjusted, it might be necessary to supplement the classroom teacher with an instructional aide.

Other decisions will appear constantly for the team, such as questions about an extended school year, participation in special events, the extent of integration into other settings, and ways to address communication, behavior, and social skills. Each consideration must be addressed with current information from all members of the team.

Coordinator for Services

The multiple components of an autism profile can create a programming nightmare if services aren't coordinated well. I have great sympathy for classroom teachers and parents who have multiple professional disciplines providing supplemental services in a vacuum while they attempt to put it all together. In addition, the parent or teacher is also usually struggling with his own responsibilities.

A chasm can also appear from year-to-year in programming. A team may have all aspects under control, and then the child changes grades, schools, or settings, resulting in a new set of professionals who don't have experience with the child. A parent's worse nightmare is the constantly changing personnel who are charged with implementing her child's educational program. Techniques that work well might get lost in the transition, resulting in regression.

Communication among all members of a team is a critical, collective responsibility to meet an individual's needs. Brainstorming among team members also diffuses frustration for the professional who experiences difficulty implementing the child's educational program. Integrating disciplines requires a team coordinator, whose primary responsibility is to maintain a consistent channel among all team members involved in programming efforts. The coordinator should become the constant over time; a respected professional who bridges across the transitions to ensure continued progress for the child with autism. The coordinator should fill in any gaps between home and school, teacher to teacher, school to school, or professional to professional.

Often the highest level administrator or professional serves as the team coordinator, yet that person may not always be the best choice. That person might be extremely peripheral to the everyday programming, with minimal consistent interaction with the disabled child. The team coordinator needs to spend time on a regular basis with the child, as well as hold some weight in making decisions. Personal familiarity with an individual's needs, progress, and problems is critical for effective team coordination.

Team Member Responsibilities

Each team member's role varies by setting. While some responsibilities are obvious to the specific area of expertise, others evolve, consistent with an individual's personality or skills, regardless of discipline.

The chart below provides a summary of primary responsibilities by professional discipline. The chart is not inclusive, but suggests a general outline for team coordination. Other professionals may be available, such as a music therapist or behavior consultant. A sample of goals by discipline is included in Appendix 4C, page 67.

Team Members and Responsibilities

Psychologist	Psychometric tests Cognitive level Achievement level Informal behavioral observation
Speech-Language Pathologist	Receptive language level Expressive language level Pragmatic/Social level Informal behavioral observation
Occupational Therapist	Sensory integration tests Fine-motor development Informal behavioral observation
Physical Therapist	Motor movement and strength Gross-motor development Informal behavioral observation
Social Worker	General development Health history Support services for family Informal behavioral observation
Classroom Teacher	Achievement levels Academic and social skills Informal behavioral observation
Administrator	Liaison among professionals Funding/Paperwork coordination Support system for professionals Informal behavioral observation
Parent	Liaison among settings Developmental/Functional levels Informal behavioral observation
Physician	Medical and general health status Monitor medications
All Members	Behavior management Interpersonal social development

Summary Comments

➡ The multifaceted syndrome of autism requires a myriad of professionals who may provide services in conjunction with the disability. Coordinating the work of several disciplines requires a collaborative team effort.

➡ Team decisions are not easy within the autism spectrum. The continuum of severity in each symptom creates a unique programming puzzle for each individual. The team must maintain objectivity and balance strengths and weaknesses, evaluating and discussing both abilities and disabilities.

➡ A determination of placement is probably one of the most critical decisions a team makes. This decision establishes the environment in which programming will occur. The child's needs should drive the placement decision. One strategy that helps avoid limiting the choices is to generate all the options available and discuss advantages and disadvantages. This way, the team literally builds the placement to fit the child's needs, while being consistent with the team's options.

➡ Communication among team members should be frequent. Consistency across settings is critical to progress for the individual with autism. Everyone needs to agree on programming techniques. When controversy arises, compromise is easier to accept for short durations. While re-convening a team meeting is not convenient, a trial period may appease team members. Programming decisions do not have to be for a year. A team can meet as frequently as necessary to modify and try new options.

➡ Both access to resource professionals and training for team members contribute greatly to the confidence and comfort of the group. No one person or team has all the answers. Flexibility and creativity are important, but knowing that a team can contact another professional for ideas adds an important dimension. Reassurance that the team is working well and on the right track reduces anxiety. Minimize stress so that it doesn't become a negative factor disrupting team meetings. An outside influence or recommendation can reduce the burden of responsibility on team members who must work together. The goal of a team is to maintain a coordinated effort to ensure an individual's progress toward reaching potential.

Appendix 4A: Diagnostic Profile

Name: <u>Sam H.</u>   Age: <u>5 years 0 months</u>   Date: <u>4/xx/96</u>
Site: <u>Early Childhood Program</u>   Purpose: <u>Determine Fall IEP Goals and Placement</u>

Language

1.   Articulation: few sounds in error — /l,r/
2.   Syntax
     a.   pronoun reversals and confusion; uses *you / me; he / she; Sam / I*
     b.   correct grammar but simple sentence structure
3.   Semantics
     a.   delay in abstract vocabulary & concepts; vocabulary splintered; some $50 words!
          problems with prepositions, opposites, etc.
     b.   repeats things over and over
     c.   very complex, detailed, verbal output on specific topics of fascination
     d.   asks questions incessantly
4.   Pragmatics
     a.   poor eye contact
     b.   doesn't share personal information
     c.   won't initiate spontaneous speech
     d.   talks like a robot (monotone)
     e.   not aware of others around him

Behavior

1.   Won't follow directions
2.   Won't attend in group; gets up and wanders away
3.   Disrupts group by talking out of turn
4.   Screams and cries when he can't finish what he wants
5.   Tantrums and flaps arms when he has to share toys
6.   Sorts and lines up the blocks instead of building
7.   Refuses to answer or respond when his name is called
8.   Refuses to eat snack, but sniffs and plays with it
9.   Covers his ears when he walks down the hall
10. Fixates on dangerous things, but has no reaction to pain

Academic Achievement/Cognitive Skills

1.   Reads everything in sight, but won't answer any questions
2.   Good letter and number recognition, but no one-to-one correspondence
3.   Recognizes colors, but inconsistent
4.   Can tell time to the minute
5.   Good vocabulary for identifying objects, counting, and ABCs
6.   Uncooperative or inconsistent on cognitive tests

Motor

1.   Advanced gross-motor skills
2.   Physically very active; won't sit still; always rubbing
3.   Won't write his name or color in the lines, but reproduces drawings in great detail
4.   Becomes aggressive if you try to assist him physically

Appendix 4B: Educational Goals

I. Sam will improve functional language abilities to approximate an age-appropriate level.

    A. To improve pragmatic skills for more effective interaction:
1. Sam will decrease robotic/monotone speech and increase his inflection to a more appropriate range with 80% consistency as judged appropriate by his teachers.
2. Sam will answer questions appropriately about people and objects in the environment with 80% accuracy.
3. During group sharing, Sam will answer personal questions appropriately and offer personal information (i.e., name, address, and phone number) with 80% accuracy.
4. Sam will decrease asking inappropriate questions to a maximum of 10 per day.

    B. To increase receptive and expressive language:
1. Sam will demonstrate comprehension and use of a minimum of 10 terms in the following conceptual/abstract vocabulary areas with 80% accuracy:
    a. spatial prepositions (e.g., *on, under, above,* and *behind)*
    b. size concepts (e.g., *large, small,* and *medium)*
    c. opposites (e.g., *on/off, full/empty,* and *late/early)*
2. Sam will appropriately use the female and male gender specific pronouns and vocabulary of *boy-girl, man-woman, he-she, his-her,* and *Mr.-Mrs.* with 80% accuracy in spontaneous speech.

    C. To monitor and correct articulation inconsistencies in spontaneous speech.

II. Sam will improve social interaction skills to approximate age-appropriate levels.

    A. To increase appropriate classroom participation and decrease inappropriate behavior:
1. During group instruction, Sam will sit quietly and attend to the teacher with 80% accuracy.
2. During group instruction, Sam will raise his hand to make requests, answer questions, or offer comments 80% of the time.
3. When given a one- to three-step direction, Sam will comply appropriately with 80% accuracy.
4. During play time and group instruction, Sam will wait his turn appropriately 80% of the time.
5. When moving from one activity to the next, Sam will make the transition appropriately 3 out of 5 times per day.

    B. To increase appropriate pragmatic behaviors:
1. Sam will demonstrate appropriate use of social terms (i.e., *please, thank-you, hi,* and *bye)* 60% of the time.
2. Sam will maintain appropriate eye contact when speaking to another person for a minimum of 2 seconds 75% of the time.
3. Sam will initiate and maintain appropriate social contact with a peer for a minimum of 2 minutes at least once a day.

III. Sam will improve academic skills from a pre-kindergarten level to a late kindergarten level.

    A.   To improve reading comprehension skills:
        1. After hearing a story, Sam will answer correctly 4 out of 5 *wh-* questions about the story.
        2. After hearing a portion of a story, Sam will use critical thinking skills to predict outcomes, draw conclusions, and make inferences with 80% accuracy.
        3. After reading a story, Sam will answer correctly 4 out of 5 *wh-* questions about the story.
        4. After reading a story, Sam will use critical thinking skills to predict outcomes, draw conclusions, and make inferences with 80% accuracy.

    B.   To improve math skills:
        1. Given a group of objects, Sam will use one-to-one correspondence to count with 80% accuracy.
        2. Given two groups of objects, Sam will identify *more than, less than, equal to*, and *zero* with 80% accuracy.

IV. Sam will improve his fine-motor skills to approximate an age-appropriate level.

    A.   To improve eye-hand coordination:
        1. When given a series of geometric shapes drawn on paper, Sam will cut within ¼" of the line with 80% accuracy.
        2. When given crayons and black line drawings, Sam will color within ¼" of the line with 80% accuracy.

    B.   To improve writing skills:
        1. Given alphabet letters, Sam will trace them within recognizable limits with 90% accuracy.
        2. Given alphabet letters, Sam will copy them within recognizable limits with 90% accuracy.
        3. Sam will write alphabet letters within recognizable limits with 90% accuracy.

Placement Options

    1. Regular kindergarten with a one-on-one aide and a resource room (LD)

    2. Self-contained learning disabled/cross categorical classroom with integration to a regular kindergarten classroom

    3. Supplemental service options:
        a. personal aide
        b. speech therapy
        c. learning disability services
        d. occupational therapy
        e. behavioral consultant
        f. social worker/counselor
        g. psychologist

    4. Goal responsibility: Be flexible! Who can best address needs?

Appendix 4C: Sample Goals from a Team Perspective

Speech-Language Pathologist

I. Semantic Language Development
   A. Receptive and expressive vocabulary
   B. Conceptual language: concrete vs. abstract
   C. Verbal problem-solving and reasoning

II. Pragmatic Language Development
   A. Develop appropriate nonverbal social-interaction skills
   B. Develop verbal social-interaction skills
   C. Develop supplemental aspects of verbal language

Parent

I. Self-Care Skills
   A. Acceptance of varying food textures
   B. Improve falling asleep and sleep maintenance behaviors
   C. Toileting

II. Interpersonal, Home, and Community Skills
   A. Improve physical interaction with smaller children
   B. Shopping behavior
   C. Tolerance for clothing of varying textures

Occupational Therapist

I. Fine-Motor Skills
   A. Accurate coloring when given parameters
   B. Recognizable writing
   C. Improve scissors skills

II. Sensory Integration
   A. Decrease tactile defensiveness
   B. Address issues of sensory hypersensitivity

Teacher

I. Academic Skills
   A. Improve verbal/reading comprehension and attention
   B. Process and respond appropriately to wh- questions
   C. Demonstrate application of basic math concepts

II. Classroom Social-Interaction Skills
   A. Turn taking and waiting
   B. Transition between activities
   C. Peer interactions
   D. Acceptance of physical assistance

Chapter 5
Communication Intervention

For language to have any meaning one must be able to relate to it. For me, when the directness of relating is too great, the walls go up ... the stress of direct, emotionally loaded communication either blocks the brain's ability to retrieve all or any of the words needed to speak a fluent sentence or won't allow the process of articulation to begin, leaving the words echoing within the speaker's head.

Donna Williams
Nobody Nowhere

Communication with someone — anyone — continued to be a problem. I often sounded abrasive and abrupt. In my head I knew what I wanted to say but the words never matched my thoughts.

Temple Grandin
Emergence: Labeled Autistic

Normal Communication

Communication is a critical skill for independent functioning in today's world. The ability to receive information, attach meaning to the auditory stimulus, and express an appropriate response is a very complex process that is often taken for granted by the average person. It is when the process doesn't work effectively that people take note of significant differences. It is also a source of intense frustration for the individual who cannot engage in a normal communication process.

Language is defined by its component parts:

- phonology (rules for sound usage and production)
- morphology (smallest units of meaning in language)
- semantics (study of word meanings)
- syntax (grammatic rules of structure)
- pragmatics (social context of use)

Within autism, the areas of phonology and syntax are not significantly problematic, although there may be delays. But if the child is verbal, the stereotyped patterning behaviors of autism usually result in excellent reproduction of sounds and sentence structures. Occasionally a child with autism requires intervention specifically for motor production of a sound or for a syntactic group of words, such as personal pronouns, but in general, morphology, syntax, and phonology are intact for verbal children with autism.

Primary areas of language impairment within autism include semantics, especially as semantic language becomes more abstract (e.g., concepts, problem solving, and reasoning), and pragmatics. Idioms, colloquialisms, cultural and regional deviations, and peer level nuances all contribute to the challenge for an individual with autism. In order to understand messages, the child must process subtleties along with the actual words spoken.

The communication process requires a sender, a message, and a receiver. It implies interaction between two people who share an idea or thought. Several physiological systems of intricate coordination are involved. While most communication exchange occurs with minimal problems, a glitch anywhere in the system can compromise the process significantly.

Within autism, several neurological differences can interfere with the communication process. The sensory differences in responding to stimuli may distort input received. For example, a hypersensitivity in hearing may result in a roar of noise that is painful and overwhelming, blocking out any attention to specific sounds or words. If the person's cortex is not aroused and receptive to stimuli, his brain may not actually receive the stimuli to decode. The anxiety created by a new situation or stress of relating may prevent the person from actually processing the language message. Donna Williams wrote that it was very hard to understand what people said. "I was too busy adjusting to the new surroundings and new person, both at once, and to the feelings of being observed, as well." (*Somebody Somewhere*, 1994)

Receptive Communication

Receptive comprehension involves the ability to understand or attach meaning to a verbal stimulus. One of the initial communication goals with individuals who have autism is to ensure receptive language comprehension. It is critical that auditory stimuli received become more than patterned background noise to children with autism. They need to perceive messages embedded within a language code system.

Donna Williams (1992) related that the first time she realized there was meaning in verbal language was when she heard it through a radio. The stress of relating to people was removed and her neurological system was calm. She recognized a couple of words she knew among all the other sounds. Her ears perked up and she listened more carefully, listening for meaning or words she recognized. Donna said it was a revelation to her! Until then, she had no idea that the sound surrounding her contained messages.

Receptive language tends to develop in a young child through concrete experiences. For a child with autism, the visual-motor system strongly influences understanding of the world. If the child can experience an item through her senses (e.g., touch it, smell it, taste it, see it, or move it), then the item becomes meaningful in a functional sense. The challenge is to link the physical understanding of an item to the auditory sound, or language label, representing it. A child with autism may not respond when you verbally offer a favorite toy. However, if you show the child the toy, she will scramble for it. Building receptive understanding of language terms is difficult.

Once concrete understanding of language begins to develop in the child with autism, professionals and parents begin to relax and presume the communication developmental process is underway and will continue. However, a major chasm exists for the child with autism as language changes from concrete terminology to abstract terms. Many ideas cannot be presented concretely. We use language to code and express things like emotions, thoughts, theories, and philosophies. Receptive language challenges continue to present themselves throughout life, especially for the individual with autism. Reasoning, understanding relationships and feelings, and problem solving are examples of language-based concepts that confuse and confound even high-functioning people with autism. The mystery of understanding abstract ideas receptively is compounded when interaction and verbal demands are added.

Expressive Communication

Verbal

Autism is a unique disability in one aspect of expressive language. In most individuals, we presume receptive understanding of language in expressive output. That is, if a person talks about a topic, we presume the person understands what she's saying. But in autism, the echolalic characteristic creates an unusual situation. It is not unusual to have an individual who can produce beautifully expressive language without understanding a word of the message.

Echolalia functions like a tape recorder. The person with autism hits a "record" button in his brain when he hears information. He does not process or attach meaning to the verbal stimuli, and no pictures or images are triggered in his brain. When a key prompt is heard later, the person pushes the "play" button and recites the whole verbal monologue.

A good example of this phenomena occurred when I began working in a diagnostic preschool setting. After a long holiday weekend, the teachers were asking children what they had done over the weekend vacation. One boy immediately began telling the group about a camping trip. He explained in great detail how the beds folded out, how the bathroom worked, how the stove and refrigerator were hooked up, and what foods they had eaten. The educational team was in awe of his language and wondered why he was in the center for diagnosis! Later, his mother clarified that the family had never been camping and they didn't own a camper. Further research on the mother's part turned up a neighbor who had a new camper and had been on a trip that weekend. The boy had overheard the whole conversation, recorded it under the prompt "What did you do this weekend?" and played it back for us! We were so impressed with the language structures that we forgot a cardinal rule: do reality checks!

Reality checks are critical within autism. Teachers and clinicians should explore meaning within any language recitation with objects, pictures, and questions. Monitor verbal language output consistently for receptive comprehension. Methods to examine and increase meaningfulness are expanded upon later in this chapter.

Speech delivery style is another aspect of verbal expression. When a person talks to share factual data, his speech can lack inflectional variation and modulation. The result is a flat, monotone quality, similar to synthesized or artificially produced speech. The speaker can sound void of emotion or sincerity due to the poor production style. A common misperception about people with autism is that they lack emotions due to their robotic speech delivery. Of course, the opposite can also occur. I have experienced children with autism who speak with exaggeration to the point of sounding melodramatic. The remediation goal, in any case, is to modify verbal production to a functional delivery style.

Nonverbal

A review of the literature suggests that approximately 40% of people with autism remain mute. The inability to produce speech is probably due to an oral-motor apraxia. When verbal output is not an option for expressing one's thoughts, other options for sending messages must be explored. Augmentative alternative communication (AAC) methods have been used within autism for decades. Research from the 1950s documents ways of teaching sign language, using picture-pointing responses, and alphabet spelling boards. Yet professionals have often been frustrated by the inability to establish reliable, interactive communication when the verbal output system fails. Many speech-language pathologists advocate a total communication approach through the early years of intervention to ensure that all modalities are receiving stimuli and have the opportunity to attempt programming a response. Total communication entails the use of both speech and sign language. The individual receives an auditory model for speech production that is supported by a visual signed system of gestures. Many children with autism seem to read and respond to signs for message input, yet the number of those who use signs to send messages is more limited.

Picture communication boards have also been used extensively. Picture communication boards vary in complexity and form. Some boards use actual photographs, while others rely on abstract line drawings to symbolize items. Picture communication systems range in complexity from cards with one picture per card, to pages with multiple pictures in category units. Technology has introduced computer-based systems that can scan rows of icons and the individual merely stops the scanner at the appropriate item. These systems can be programmed to meet a person's unique needs. Many also have speech synthesizers to provide a verbal model for both the sender and receiver.

Alphabet spelling techniques have also been used over time. Several individuals with autism were placed on typewriters and could motor program a finger typing response when their oral-motor coordination did not work accurately. A recent modification in an alphabet spelled system is facilitated communication. Facilitated communication originated in Australia with individuals who had neuro-motor disabilities. The idea was to provide an easier neuro-motor response for people with intact mental capacity but compromised motor function. The technique was brought to the United States and introduced with a focused emphasis for individuals with autism. While debate continues about the specific technique of facilitated communication, it does provide another option for augmentative communication.

If a child with autism cannot accomplish verbal speech production, then nonverbal options must be explored. Initiate augmentative and alternative communication options as soon as possible to ensure a method for reciprocal interaction. Early systems should be very functional and concrete. A sample progression for communication systems might be the following:

1. objects
2. photographs
3. colored pictures
4. black and white line drawings
5. printed words

Printed words should accompany all steps in the sequence listed above. For example, objects in the environment can have labels on them so the child can begin associating the objects with their labels. The goal is to work toward a print system. Many electronic communication systems use picture symbol icons if a child has not yet mastered reading.

Always encourage automatic speech and simple, single words, even for the primarily nonverbal child. Simple requests (e.g., *yes, no, eat, potty, stop,* and *help*) contain a great deal of manipulative power in the environment. A child who can say intelligible representations of simple power words should be encouraged to speak these words, even if he uses an alternative communication system for more extensive interaction.

Emphasize oral-motor exercises to encourage speech with all children who are nonverbal. A child's neurological system can be delayed in maturation and myelinization within the syndrome of autism and PDD. Stimulating an immature system, regardless of chronological age, may facilitate progress for single-word production. My experience supports an increase in speaking single words when augmentative systems are introduced because programming the message is slowed down. The resulting slower pace allows the child to motor program verbalizations that could not be accomplished previously. Examples of goals and techniques follow in the next section.

Communication Deficits within Autism

Four of the major challenges in the area of communication within autism are listed below, followed by discussion (pragmatic language is addressed in Chapter 9). Each challenge is explained, followed by sample goals for intervention objectives.

Communication Challenges
1. Oral-Motor Programming
2. Automatic Speech
3. Echolalia
4. Meaningfulness Ratio

1. Oral-Motor Programming

Statistics suggest that 40% of individuals with autism are non-verbal due to difficulty in programming their muscles for oral speech. Oral apraxia was listed as a characteristic earlier (Autism Facts, page 15). The intricate neurological coordination required to produce speech is often taken for granted, yet delays and differences in neurological development can greatly impact the ability to produce speech. Focus intervention on direct stimulation for oral-motor development by using a consistent exercise program. Exercises should involve visual-motor modalities to enhance attention for the child with autism. Visual-motor stimulation may also facilitate an increased frequency in practicing the exercises. Examples of exercise goals are listed on page 74.

Oral-Motor Exercise Goals

I. Encourage a voluntary, controlled breath stream to provide an air supply for speech.

   A. Have the child blow a party favor so that it unfurls all the way. Work to have the child blow and unfurl the party favor and hold it unfurled (straight) for several seconds.

   B. Have the child blow bubbles. Begin with a bubble pipe to stimulate the lip area. Gradually move toward blowing bubbles with the bubble wand, without using lip stimulation.

   C. Have cotton ball races across the table or floor. Gradually increase the distance so the child has to increase his breath supply and sustain it for longer time periods.

   D. Have the child blow out a candle or multiple candles.

      Note: A word of caution when using candles and fire. The visual stimulation of candles is very motivating and concrete to sustain children's attention, but close, careful supervision is necessary to ensure safety.

   E. Have the child blow a whistle or horn. Increase gradually to having the child use a controlled, sustained airflow by prolonging the sound or whistle. Again, the lip stimulation assists to innervate the breath stream.

   F. Have the child blow up balloons. You may need to loosen or stretch the balloon until the child can attain the air volume to initiate the blowing process.

II. Encourage a voluntary, voiced air stream to provide sound for speech production.

   A. Have the child blow into a kazoo. Air alone will make no noise; the child must voice or hum with the air to achieve a noise. The kazoo provides lip stimulation to help innervate the oral speech mechanism.

   B. Have the child hum into a bottle, can, or other resonating object. Encourage him to prolong the sound so he can hear and feel the vibration, both of which might be calming for him.

   C. Have the child imitate or make various environmental noises. You can pair this activity with receptive or expressive vocabulary goals, such as determining what sound various animals or environmental objects make.

   D. Use a stopwatch or timer to see how long the child can imitate and prolong various vowel sounds. Use friendly competition to provide a model. Race to see who can hold the sound the longest.

III. Encourage voluntary production of various phonemes to practice producing various sounds for speech production. Pair production of various phonemes with motor movement and activity.

A. Incorporate production of "p" into a theme lesson with focus on that sound. For example, sing "Pop Goes the Weasel" and have the students all jump up and shout "pop" during the appropriate place in the song. Have popcorn as a snack. As an activity, the children could act out being the popcorn. They can jump up and say "pop."

B. Use M&M's® as reinforcers or as a snack while teaching the production of "m." Each time the child eats the candy, ask him how it tastes to elicit a "mmmm" while rubbing his stomach.

C. Production of "b" can focus on various blowing activities in conjunction with a pretend birthday party. Party favors, balloons, bubbles, horns, and candles all require blowing.

2. Automatic Speech

A task which has been done over and over again becomes somewhat automatic to the neurological system. Programming the skill takes less conscious energy if it has been done repeatedly in the same pattern. Certain speech productions can acquire similar neurological status. Phrases, songs, or certain words that are said repetitively become fairly automatic and do not require a great deal of conscious energy. Certain meditation rites actually use a *mantra*, or short phrase, repeated over and over again as a technique to relax, calm the system, and decrease anxiety.

For children with autism, communication provokes anxiety. The task of programming speech from an idea in the mind into the linguistic code and then into the neurological system can be overwhelming. As a result, the degree of conscious effort required results in avoidance. The child is thus denied the practice of engaging in frequent verbal interaction.

Automatic speech is a nice interim technique to encourage the child with autism to innervate the neurological system, yet keep the stress of interaction to a minimum. The secret is to use pre-generated language. The child can practice producing words and sentences without worrying about which words to choose or the rhythm or rate at which to speak. Automatic speech can also have the added positive effect of calming down a child with autism because of the repetitive pattern. Sample goals for promoting automatic speech are listed on page 76.

Automatic Speech Goals

I. Encourage automatic speech through rote recitation and songs.

   A. Model reciting nursery rhymes, the *Pledge of Allegiance*, counting numbers, the alphabet, the days of week, the months of year, and choral poems and practice them consistently as part of a daily routine. The child with autism may only observe and not recite, but will usually begin to participate gradually.

   B. Finger plays, songs, songs with actions or movement are excellent language models to encourage neurological coordination for expressive speech.

   C. Musical videos, tapes, CDs, commercial jingles, and other music stimuli may be calming and reinforcing.

II. Encourage automatic speech by using simple words with manipulative power in the environment that have an immediate impact on the student.

   A. Model and consistently encourage using environmentally manipulative words such as *yes, no, toilet, water, hi, bye, please, thank you, eat,* and *stop*.

   B. Simplify verbal models to include only key words to facilitate comprehension, as well as repetition by the child.

   C. Exaggerated inflection and sing-songy verbalizations may enhance the child's attention on auditorially presented information. Giving directions the same way, in a routine, or preceded by a similar prompt may be less threatening.

3. Echolalia and Meaningfulness Ratio

Echoing language generated by another person is a normal step in language development. Parents and professionals provide a language model for the child to imitate. Once children have practiced producing language through imitation, they progress to generating original, meaningful utterances.

Echolalia is a high-frequency characteristic within autism. The stress of interaction tends to significantly delay and compromise the process of moving from echolalia to spontaneous, original speech. Donna Williams explained in *Nobody Nowhere* (1992):

> As an echolalic child, I did not understand the use of words because I was in too great a state of stress and fear to hear anything other than patterned sound. The need to hide the fear is such that not even the face is allowed to show it. The comprehension of words works as a progression, depending on the amount of stress caused from fear and the stress of directly relating.

While echolalia is often viewed as a negative characteristic, it actually presents several positive features. The three features are listed below and then explained further.

```
┌─────────────────────────────────────────────────────────────┐
│                 Positive Features of Echolalia                │
│                                                               │
│   1. Echolalia indicates the ability to produce speech.       │
│                                                               │
│   2. Echolalia indicates the child is making progress in      │
│      language development through attaining the imitation     │
│      stage.                                                   │
│                                                               │
│   3. Echolalia indicates an awareness of conversational       │
│      turn-taking.                                             │
└─────────────────────────────────────────────────────────────┘
```

First, a child with autism who engages in echolalia is consciously using the speech mechanism. Speech is being produced through stimulation of the child's neurological system for oral-motor production. Each time the child echoes, he is practicing producing specific sounds and words.

Second, normal children progress through a modeling stage in their speech-language development. The stage suggests an awareness of auditory stimuli as a pleasant and intriguing sensation. Echolalia allows the child to try speaking with minimal effort on the language-generating areas of the brain.

Third, a child who echoes is demonstrating an awareness of taking turns in conversation. The adult talks. Then, the child realizes it is her turn to talk, but is so stressed from the anxiety of relating that she can't think of anything to say. Consequently, she says what she just heard. Then the pressure is off, and it is the adult's turn to talk again. The child has marked her turn in the conversation.

The obvious next step is to move the child forward from echolalic, non-meaningful speech to spontaneous, meaningful speech. Once the child's anxiety decreases, the goal is to remain calm enough to generate meaningful language instead of echoing what was heard before. As parents and professionals, we often try to take too large a step with the child with autism.

People often rely on trite, pre-generated phrases in stressful or awkward situations. The salient feature is that the phrase, even though not original, is used appropriately; the words are meaningful within the specific situation. The child with autism should be allowed to pull phrases from her repertoire of language previously stored. The first step is for her to be calm enough during interaction to retrieve appropriate phrases from her stored language bank. A later step can be to generate original comments or questions.

The goal is not to extinguish echolalia, but to shape echolalia from non-meaningful to meaningful utterances. A relatively easy method to evaluate the shaping process can be accomplished using what I call a Meaningfulness Ratio. A Meaningfulness Ratio is derived from charting a conversational sample of a child with autism. First, decide whether each utterance was related to the conversation or was inappropriate. The decision has nothing to do with accuracy or correctness of the response. It is only concerned with whether the comment made sense in the situation. Then, determine the percentage of meaningful (or non-meaningful) responses by dividing the number of comments in that category by the total number of the child's comments. An example conversation is charted below.

Conversation Sample	Meaningfulness Ratio	
	Meaningful	Non-Meaningful
Adult: What is this?		
Child: What is this?		1
Adult: Do you know what it is, Ashley?		
Child: A pencil.	1	
Adult: What do we do with a pencil?		
Child: A pencil.		1
Adult: Pencil does what?		
Child: Write.	1	
Adult: Nice. Good answer!		
Child: Good answer.		1
Adult: What is this?		
Child: What is this?		1
Adult: This is . . .		
Child: This is . . .		1
Adult: Ashley, I have a piece of . . .		
Child: Piece of paper.	1	
Adult: Yes. Paper.		
Child: Paper.		1
Adult: You write on paper with a pencil.		
Child: What is this? What is this?		1

The Meaningfulness Ratio Tally would look like this, resulting in an informal impression that 30% of verbal utterances are meaningful, or 70% of utterances are non-meaningful.

Meaningfulness Ratio

Meaningful	Non-Meaningful
|||	̶H̶H̶ ||

78

The goal is not to reduce speech by 70% through extinguishing echolalic or non-meaningful responses. The goal is to maintain the verbal output level, but work to increase meaningfulness. Shaping echolalia into meaningful interaction will transfer tallies from the non-meaningful column to meaningful. Another clinical example might help to illustrate the shaping process.

A first-grade boy with autism had a routine to get his lunchbox, line up along the wall, walk to the cafeteria, and eat lunch with his peers. However, today his mother was coming to pick him up from the cafeteria for a doctor's appointment. After the appointment, she was taking him to his favorite place for lunch and bringing him back to school.

The change in routine was anxiety provoking, as demonstrated through an increase in echolalia. The teacher gave the direction to line up for lunch and the boy started echoing the routine. "Get your lunch and line up. Get your lunch. Get your lunch." The teacher asked what was wrong to break the non-meaningful echoes. The boy replied, "I don't have a lunch. No lunch. Can't line up. No lunch." The teacher told the boy to line up anyway, so he continued echoing, but with increased volume and agitation.

An aide intervened and asked the boy what day it was. He replied immediately. Then, she asked who was coming to school today. The boy answered, "My mom." "Why is your mom coming?" The aide and the boy continued to talk through the situation. What was a continuing spiral of marks in the non-meaningful column while behavior escalated, immediately became marks in the meaningful column by refocusing the child in functional conversation.

Calculate the meaningfulness ratio periodically in various settings. The resulting number can provide insight to the child's comfort level for interaction with various people or settings. Remember that echolalia is a positive sign that requires intervention to move the language development along. My best success story was a little girl who progressed from an echolalic phase of 20% meaningfulness to 85% meaningfulness within two years!

4. Abstract Language

Language development proceeds from concrete, functional noun and verb classes of words into more abstract vocabulary. For the child with autism, transitions from experiential words to conceptual ideas is difficult.

Most of the readiness skills targeted during preschool years are to help the child make the jump from concrete language into abstract language. For example, basic concepts are required before any academic tasks can be introduced. Math is built on concepts such as *whole, half, equal, part, few, many, pair, add,* and *subtract.* History relies on time concepts such as *yesterday* and *tomorrow.* Everyday academic directions incorporate *left, right, top, bottom, behind, in, out,* and *above.* The list expands quickly and expectations for comprehension are prerequisite to early elementary school success.

For children with autism, language concepts that teachers and families consider relatively easy can be very confusing. For example, children with autism learn the concepts of *on* and *off* at a young age. Most of these youngsters are fascinated by turning on and off lights, buttons, and switches and watching the movement stop and start. These children have learned the terms in situational contexts. Then, a teacher gives a direction with *on the desk.* Suddenly, the child is being punished for crawling around on the floor under the teacher's desk. The child was probably looking for the switch to turn on the teacher's desk!

The child with autism can be incredibly perplexed by the simplest things within language — like why a *bat* is sometimes a stick to hit a baseball and sometimes a black animal that flies. One little girl I worked with used to request working on multiple-meaning word cards because she loved figuring out the various meanings of words.

Language demands continue to become abstract as a child with autism grows older. Problem-solving and reasoning skills should be developed at an external, functional level. You can create situations in which the student might need to request assistance or strategize alternatives. Generate all alternatives; then, evaluate them and discuss the "best" alternatives. This discussion of the process should facilitate the student's internal problem-solving and reasoning skills.

The details of life embedded within language are subtle and often missed by the person with autism. The focus on language content is so intense that the person misses the nuances. Professionals and parents need to provide direct goals and therapy in abstract language areas to facilitate independence. Life, the best teacher, provides a wealth of opportunities to teach language competence.

Life = Language

Almost everything introduced in the educational system has a language base. Teaching involves interaction through language, both receptive and expressive. Assessment evaluates a child's understanding (receptive language comprehension) and response accuracy (expressive language). Every professional and parent works through a language medium. It amazes me, therefore, to encounter communication goals on educational plans that confine language intervention to the speech-language pathologist. Furthermore, the speech pathology services provided usually average 30 minutes twice a week! A child with autism is bombarded by language every minute of every day, yet one hour per week of focused intervention should remediate deficits in the area of language?

I like to use the analogy of developing abilities in the areas of athletics and music. Consider approaching the basketball coach or band director and telling him that his students can practice for 30 minutes twice a week, and good luck in their performance against competition! Communities would be very upset if a school district restricted practice to one hour a week. Yet language skills are the basis for math, reading, science, history, and future vocations. Who will rally for intense services and practice opportunities to provide the foundation for all interaction and communication?

Professionals and parents must assume some responsibility in meeting language objectives. Every interaction becomes a teaching opportunity with the child who has autism. Artificially-created situations are not as potent for teaching or carryover of skills as the real-life environment. An understanding of language goals and methods to stimulate communicative interaction must be pervasive in a child's program.

Behavior = Nonverbal Communication

A teacher and a parent were both extremely frustrated by a child who frequently screamed when new things were introduced. They said, "If he could just tell us what was wrong, it would be so much easier." My response surprised them. I told them the child was communicating very clearly what was wrong. They weren't listening to his nonverbal behavior.

A child who screams when new items are presented is reacting through a hypersensitive sensory system. The behavior was a nonverbal message that certain items were anxiety provoking. The teacher and parent needed to recognize the nonverbal communication and begin analyzing

81

its intent. For example, which items does a child not cry in response to? Which items seem to trigger more intense crying? Which items does a child seem to accept quicker? Does the reaction vary with different people, at different times of the day, or in different settings? In short, 1) why is the behavior occurring; and 2) what is the message behind the behavior?

Children with autism are not very proficient in communicating an accurate reflection of their feelings verbally. However, their behavior is often a very accurate reflection of their neurological state. It's important for families and professionals to pay attention to nonverbal communication signs. Another case example illustrates this point.

> A five-year-old boy became very verbal in small group instruction, distracting the teacher and other children. When the teacher talked, the boy began reciting the alphabet, singing songs, or echoing the teacher. When an aide quieted him down, he appeared to tune out and did not answer any questions or respond to his name. When he was allowed to talk simultaneously with the teacher, he responded accurately.

> Tactile modification techniques were tried without success. The introduction of stimulation toys were not effective in keeping him quiet or focused. A suggestion was made that perhaps he needed auditory stimulation to remain focused. He was given a small, battery operated chicken that cheeped only when it was in contact with the boy's skin.

> The boy loved the chicken and the "cheep, cheep" seemed to be enough to keep him focused. His attention was good and his responses were accurate, but the teacher was fairly annoyed with the cheeping. She was encouraged to give it some time to see if she and the other students could desensitize to it and eventually fade it out. After a few days, the teacher admitted that she wasn't noticing the "cheeping" as much.

> My observation added a new perspective. When the chicken was cheeping, the child was having trouble focusing and he needed stimulation to stay calm and attentive. When the chicken was quiet, he was calm and paying attention to the stimuli. Rather than tune out the cheeping, I encouraged the teacher to tune in to the cheeping. If the toy kept cheeping incessantly, it meant the child had reached his threshold and was nearing a behavioral outburst. The chicken provided an internal reading of the child's neurological state. When the chicken wasn't calming the child down, the teacher needed to excuse him for a walk or to go swing before his nonverbal behavior escalated.

Summary Comments

➡ Communication implies interaction, a potentially threatening and anxiety-provoking situation for the individual with autism. Stress relating to interaction can minimize communicative effectiveness.

➡ Receptive language skill is the ability to understand spoken language. Expressive language skill is the ability to produce an appropriate message or response. With autism, receptive understanding cannot be assumed within expressive output!

➡ Apraxia occurs in approximately 40% of individuals with autism. If speaking is not an option for communication, explore other methods of communication, such as sign language, picture communication boards, typing, and electronic computer devices. However, parents and professionals shouldn't abandon verbal stimulation until a child is in upper elementary school because of neurological delays consistent with the syndrome of autism.

➡ Expressive communication for the child with autism must be shaped from non-meaningful to meaningful. The first steps must be to assure the child's comfort during interaction to reduce his anxiety. The next level of intervention is to encourage automatic speech responses the child can use when pressured. Later stages will address the child's spontaneous generation of verbal utterances. Language objectives must also move from concrete, experiential activities to abstract concepts.

➡ Successful intervention for communication deficits must be a shared responsibility. Success will not be facilitated by isolated, sterile services.

➡ Read the nonverbal behavioral signs of communication to determine messages that the child's neurological system is attempting to send.

Chapter 6
Sensory System Differences

There is a mechanism in the inner ear that controls the body's balance and integrates visual and vestibular input. Autistic children often have reduced nystagmus. It is as if their bodies were demanding more spinning as a kind of corrective factor in an immature nervous system.

Temple Grandin
Emergence: Labeled Autistic

Sensory Systems

Environmental stimuli can be very disturbing to someone with autism. Research suggests that within the syndrome of autism, the sensory systems respond to stimuli differently. The nature of reaction can be a hypersensitive over-response to stimuli, or a hyposensitive under-response to stimuli. All six major sensory systems, diagrammed below, can be affected within autism.

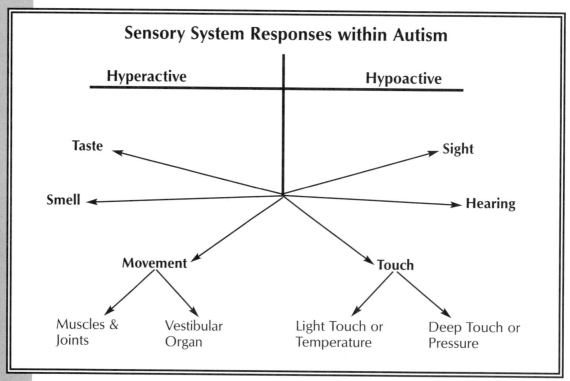

Many of the behavioral outbursts and poor attention problems within autism are directly attributable to the sensory system response to stimuli present. For example, one explanation for their picky eating habits is probably their hyperactive smell and taste responses. Certain tastes and smells are intolerable.

Sensory systems gradually desensitize over time. Individuals with autism build up a tolerance through exposure. Part of programming is to acknowledge the legitimacy of children's responses, yet also assist in developing a tolerance to particular sensory stimuli. One such technique is Auditory Integration Therapy (AIT), which gradually desensitizes an individual's auditory system to certain sounds through controlled, consistent exposure.

CLOSE TO HOME JOHN McPHERSON

Ultra-sensitive car alarms.

The challenge for those living or working with individuals with autism is to assess their sensory differences. Due to the biochemical nature of autism, sensory system responses may change from day to day. Also, a child may respond to some auditory stimuli in a hyperactive manner (e.g., bells, whistle, and sirens) and other auditory stimuli (e.g., a voice) in a hypoactive way. This lack of obvious patterns results in little or no warning preceding a disruptive outburst, as in this CLOSE TO HOME cartoon by John McPherson.

The answer for caregivers lies in learning to read the child's nonverbal, neurological warning signs.

Neurological Connection

The quotation from Temple Grandin at the beginning of this chapter provides a clue to the common self-stimulatory behaviors within autism. The rhythmic, repetitive motor movements stimulate the vestibular system. Many verbal individuals within the autistic spectrum have told professionals that the self-stimulatory characteristics help them calm down. What is the connection between the two? The neurological chain, illustrated in the simplified diagram on page 86, explains the connection.

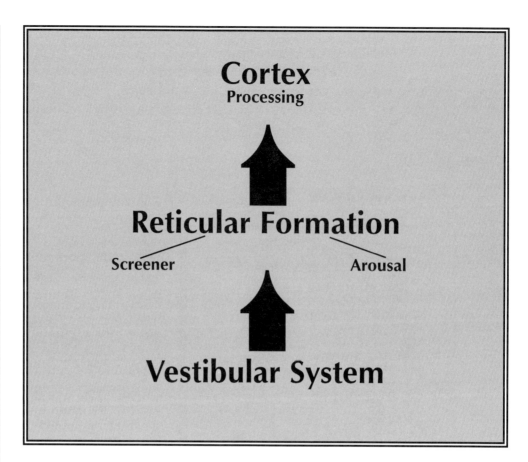

The vestibular system is located in the inner ear. Proprioceptive stimulation in the vestibular system initiates a transfer of neurological stimuli through the brainstem into a structure called the reticular formation.

The reticular formation has two important responsibilities. The first is to function as a sensory screen or gate for incoming sensory stimuli. Stimuli that require higher-level processing are sent on to the cortex for interpretation of meaning. Lower-level sensory processing can occur without involving the cortex. For example, auditory background noise, such as a fan blowing or papers rustling, does not require interpretation from the cortex. However, a teacher's voice presenting information needs to be sent to the cortex for language decoding and interpretation.

The second function of the reticular formation is to arouse the cortex and alert it to incoming sensory information. The reticular formation is the switch to wake up the brain and tell it to get ready to process sensory information being sent up. The cortex alertness and response to sensory stimuli is controlled by the reticular formation's neurological signals.

Once the cortex is aroused, processing can occur. Processing entails attaching meaning to stimuli received. The brain's ability to think and act logically on information received is dependent upon the information getting to it, via the reticular formation. In autism, the vestibular system appears to be hypoactive, requiring a great deal of stimuli to work appropriately. Without intense proprioceptive (movement) stimulation, the vestibular system doesn't innervate the reticular formation. The reticular formation has to be stimulated to screen information and arouse the cortex to incoming stimuli. A domino effect occurs when the neurological sequence is initiated.

The end result is that intense vestibular stimulation is the key to processing in the brain. There is a direct neurological connection between a child's rocking and the ability to pay attention and learn. A teacher who tells a child with autism to stop flapping his hands may be telling him indirectly to turn off his brain and stop processing information. Insisting on "quiet hands" may result in a switched-off brain.

There is another biochemical component within neurology that seems to play a part within autism. When a neurological system is overwhelmed or threatened, it can trigger a hormonal response of high anxiety. The high-anxiety chemicals start pumping, resulting in behavioral outbursts when a tolerance level has been exceeded. The neurological system starts to shut down to protect itself from the aversive stimulation.

The high anxiety or stress response is true for all of us. When we have reached our threshold of anxiety, we usually engage in some activity to reduce stress. The activity will vary by individual preference. Some do strenuous physical exercise; others block everything out and allow one calming stimulus to flood the system, such as listening to music or reading a book.

When we flood a neurological system in a sustained way, endorphins are released. Endorphins are anxiety-reducing chemicals. Research shows that endorphins may be released by certain foods as well, such as chocolate and caffeine, which may explain why some people go on binges when they're stressed. The more strenuous or sustained our physical activity, the more endorphins we trigger. Dr. Kiyo Kitahara conducted research in Japan for some time using physical exercise to achieve effective programming for autism. Her work was based on the theory that physical exercise triggers endorphins that reduce anxiety.

The stress reduction endorphins accomplish plays a part in the neurological base to behaviors within autism. Autism is a biochemical, neurological disorder. Sensory stimulation is responded to differently, triggering aberrant chemical responses. Individuals inherently learn that they calm down and feel better when they engage in repetitive motor movements, such as self-stimulatory behaviors. Thus, self-stimulatory behaviors play a double positive role within autism. The sustained, rhythmic, repetitive movement triggers release of calming endorphins.

It also provides vestibular stimulation to innervate the reticular formation to arouse the cortex to make sense of the world. Misunderstanding self-stimulatory activities by trying to eliminate the characteristic can result in dire behavioral consequences. A well-intentioned parent or professional may not realize that she is the trigger to an escalation in behavior.

Behavior management techniques and strategies are discussed further in Chapter 7. However, assessing and evaluating sensory system differences can help in designing successful programming. The techniques have been extensively researched and developed within the field of occupational therapy by A. Jean Ayres. The area of sensory integration can have a dramatic, positive influence on facilitating progress within autism.

Sensory Integration

A. Jean Ayres (1979), an occupational therapist, defined sensory integration as "the neurological process that organizes sensation from one's own body and from the environment and makes it possible to use the body effectively within the environment." The ability to make sense of sensory stimuli allows an individual to function compatibly in the world. The reverse is also true. A system that cannot accurately process or understand sensory stimuli cannot function effectively.

A neurological system with sensory differences is confused. The confusion leads to sensory defensiveness. The sensory defensiveness ranges anywhere on a continuum from mild to severe.

The concept of sensory defensiveness explains behavioral disruptions. A system that is overwhelmed by sensory stimuli reacts neurologically. That neurological response may be immature, uncontrolled, and sudden, appearing without any warning or perceived explanation within the environment. It is similar to a startle or reflex response in frightened animals. Neurological anxiety blocks the ability to think and process logically.

The same concept of sensory defensiveness can be used to an advantage in educational programming. Stimulating a child's sensory system can facilitate calming the frightened child who is overwhelmed and confused by stimuli in the environment. Attempting to stimulate the sensory system in a calming manner can result in compliant, focused behavior.

The purpose of a sensory integration evaluation is to determine how an individual's sensory system responds to different stimulation. Some sensory stimuli trigger a defensive disruptive response, while other stimuli can be very calming. The sensory system response will be unique to an individual. Some examples of sensory stimulation that may be calming for individuals with autism are listed below.

Sensory Stimulation Ideas

Listening to music

Playing in tactile bins (rice or sand table)

Water play/swimming

Rocking, swinging, spinning

Walking, running

Deep-pressure massage

Watching repetitive movement
      (ceiling fan or circling music box)

Wrapping up in a blanket or sleeping bag

Sitting in a bean-bag chair

Repetitive squeezing and releasing (on forearm)

A word of caution! While there are some general principles to follow in implementing sensory integration techniques, it's important to sort out a specific individual's system. Sensory stimulation that is calming for one individual might be a defensive trigger for another. The evaluation is typically done by a certified occupational therapist, but can vary across professional settings.

The behavioral responses of individuals with autism are correlated with sensory system responses. Wilbarger & Wilbarger (1991) presented a concept connecting the sensory system with emotional responses called the Pendulum of Emotions, illustrated below.

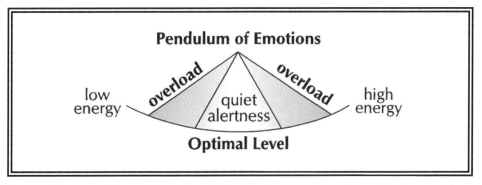

The goal is to achieve an optimal level of sensory system alertness. An overloaded sensory system can result in either a low-energy shutdown or high-energy disruption. Programming needs to work toward maintaining the optimal level to facilitate learning.

Parents and professionals often ask how much sensory integration is needed. There is no specific answer to the individuality of each person's sensory system. My best advice is offered via the Calvin and Hobbes cartoon below. The individual's behavior will let you know when the person has had enough and the system is calm, and when the person requires more to reach the optimum level.

Calvin and Hobbes   by Bill Watterson

Another question concerns the level of sensory stimulation. In young children, sensory integration may need to be very intense and can be time-consuming. Teachers often worry that sensory integration is taking away from educational input. Yet in fact, the sensory integration is stimulating the student's neurological system development. The intense sensory stimulation is allowing the student to focus and learn.

The intensity level of sensory stimulation will probably decrease over time as the child's system needs change. However, sensory differences remain an aspect of the disorder throughout life. Temple Grandin, a role model for many individuals with autism, continues to require time in her "squeeze machine." All of us need sensory "down time" to relax. The biochemical nature of autism increases the importance of calming sensory input in order to be productive. In the meantime, continue to read the nonverbal signs, as recommended in Calvin and Hobbes!

Summary Comments

➡ The neurological system of people with autism responds differently to sensory stimuli. Successful intervention requires understanding and respecting biochemical-neurological interaction. A neurological chain of events might provide the explanation underlying what appear to be unprovoked behavioral outbursts.

➡ The sensory system's hypersensitivity or hyposensitivity can result in a defensive response to environmental stimuli. The technique of sensory integration can facilitate effective focus for learning and behavioral control. Sensory integration allows the child to make sense of stimuli by stimulating the vestibular system, which in turn innervates the reticular formation and cortex. This process allows a more reasoned brain level response rather than reflexive, instinctive behavior.

➡ A second benefit of sensory integration lies in the biochemical connection. Pleasurable sensory stimulation triggers the release of endorphins, anxiety-reducing chemicals. Parents and professionals need to understand the biochemical teeter-totter with anxiety on one side and endorphins on the other. The goal is keep the anxiety level low. When the environment becomes overwhelming, introduce sensory integration to calm the system and enable the child to maintain control.

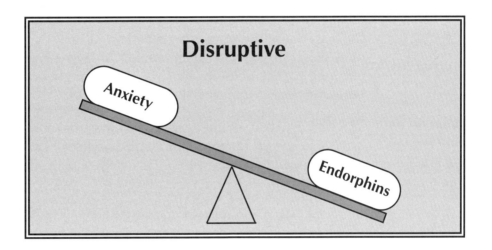

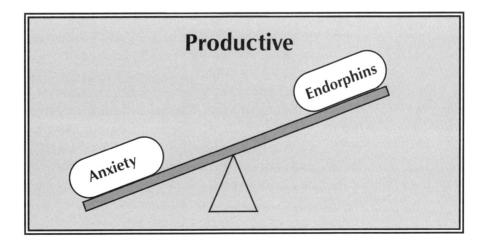

Chapter 7
Behavior Management

Try to find what triggers poor behavior and make appropriate changes in the child's daily life. Therapists and parents must be careful to differentiate between biological and behavioral causes of bad behavior.

Temple Grandin
Emergence: Labeled Autistic

Internal vs. External Triggers

Behavior is the characteristic within the syndrome of autism that seems most overwhelming to parents and professionals. Many typical behavior management techniques are not effective. Antecedent events triggering the behavior outburst escape detection. It is difficult to change or remediate behavior you don't understand! In fact, many times the well-meaning parent or professional is, unknowingly, actually pushing the button to trigger undesirable behavior.

The first aspect to understand is that most behavior within the autistic syndrome has an internal, biochemical trigger. Two quotes from high-functioning individuals with autism help explain this concept.

> The perceptual problem of deafness, muteness, and blindness are experienced as very real. They are, nevertheless, caused by extreme stress, brought on by an inability to cope with emotion. Perhaps this very real perception and the behavior it leads to are caused by oversensitivity triggering protective chemical or hormonal responses in the brain.
>
> Donna Williams, *Nobody Nowhere*

> "Panic anxiety" caused by my being overly sensitive to input to my nervous system from tactile and auditory senses.
>
> Temple Grandin, *Emergence: Labeled Autistic*

Behavior management within educational programming and parenting has been traditionally approached from an external trigger. In other words, when a child misbehaves, he is consciously choosing to misbehave. He has external control of his behavior and chooses to test the limits and suffer the consequences. Typical behavior management approaches to misbehavior capitalize on this premise by allowing the child "time out" to think about his choice, the consequences, and alternatives.

In autism, behavior is triggered through internal biochemical responses. Overwhelming stimuli trigger anxiety. The anxiety sets off chemical, hormonal responses. The child's neurological system is in a highly aroused, agitated state and literally erupts, producing sudden, unpredictable, behavior outbursts. The child cannot control the neurological venting. She also has little warning or choice in the resulting behavior. Her body is reacting via a reflexive, neurological response to aversive or agitating stimuli. Her disruptive behavior is a means to cope with the disturbing stimulus.

Often the child with autism responds to agitating stimuli by trying to create something bigger and louder to block out the unpleasant stimulus, thus the quick and sudden escalation in behavior from the child with autism. For example, suppose a boy with autism starts rocking and hand flapping after five minutes in a language group. The teacher says, "Quiet hands and sit still." Now the boy has the added pressure of trying to calm his anxiety that is building due to auditory stimuli from the language group. Without warning, he kicks the child next to him. Then, he is punished and the teacher begins talking in his face about not kicking other children. By this time, his behavior has escalated and the teacher puts him into a restraint hold!

The alternate scenario would be for the teacher to read the nonverbal signals of anxiety climbing through the movement (hand flapping and rocking). Let the child move away from the group or take a walk to calm down and return once anxiety has diminished. If the teacher missed the signs and first noticed when the boy kicked the neighboring child, then she could have let him calm his neurological system before trying to explain the rules about acceptable behavior in the language group. The teacher could have had him take a walk, move back from the group, or go listen to music to calm down. Once the child was refocused, the teacher could have explained that kicking isn't allowed.

Effective behavior management within autism needs to address the child's internal response to stimuli. When the child's sensory system is calm, he can focus and his behavior does not interfere. As anxiety begins climbing and stimuli start to wear on him, behavioral signs become apparent. He may begin rocking, make sing-songy noises, close his eyes, or move to the perimeter. The child is communicating nonverbally that a neurological response is upsetting his internal system. The parent or teacher who persists in forcing him to remain with an activity will be rewarded with a behavioral outburst. The person who recognizes the need to calm down the child's sensory system will be rewarded with minimal behavior problems, as well as the child's trust. I'm not saying that children with autism never consciously misbehave. They're normal children who will test limits. The difference is very apparent, however.

When the child is testing limits and externally choosing behavior, there is usually eye contact and a recognition (if not a verbalization) of what the consequences will be! When the child displays normal manipulative testing, typical external behavior management is appropriate. When you aren't sure, I believe it is better to err on the side of presuming internal triggers rather than external triggers. When all else fails, it never hurts to calm a neurological system down so you can deal with a more rational organism!

Communicative Intent

A little boy with autism was giggling hysterically during reading. The aide, who understood how easily this child became sensorially overloaded, asked what was wrong. The boy typed the message, "Can't stop. Outside swing please." The aide took him outside to swing. Another teacher questioned why the aide had rewarded the boy's "bad behavior." The aide realized the child wasn't choosing to be bad; he was in sensory-triggered overload. She explained, "He needs to swing to calm down." Exactly! Vestibular movement and exercise release endorphins, which are anxiety-reducing chemicals. They are the best defense for anxiety build-up. (See Chapter 6 for more detail.)

The point of the story is to analyze behavior for communicative intent. Remember that all behavior is nonverbal communication! The child's verbal system may not be very accurate, but his neurological system communicates loudly and clearly through behavior if families and professionals learn to read his internal behavior triggers.

Much behavior within autism stems from either confusion or a need for control. Confusion results when a child doesn't comprehend or can't make sense of the sensory stimuli surrounding or bombarding him. A normal voice may be perceived as patterned, disjointed, background noise to him, with no meaning or reason in the message. The longer the aversive stimuli continues, the more his anxiety builds, eventually exceeding his neurological threshold.

A child's behavior can also be a poor attempt to control stimuli that bother him. For example, suppose a child with autism perceives others' speech as an aversive, annoying, background noise that won't stop. He generates a noise (sustained screaming) bigger than the other noise. The noise the child makes doesn't bother him because he is in control of it and using it to calm himself by blocking out the aversive stimulus.

A key to behavior management is to play detective, seeking the internal behavioral trigger. It is critical to move beyond the symptom of the child's behavior. Don't treat the symptom, intervene on the trigger. A couple of examples may help to clarify.

A very bright, first-grade boy with autism had done well in a regular classroom in school until about the sixth week, when he began smearing his feces in the restroom. His behavior then escalated to pulling down his pants during math and reading, and eliminating and smearing his feces in the classroom. Needless to say, peer and teacher interaction became negative quickly!

The school hired a behavior consultant. The consultant talked with the boy and generated charts which were posted in the restroom and classroom with rules — the *do's* and *don'ts*. Contingency rewards were also listed. The specialist developed a very operant, external behavior management plan that had absolutely no effect on the boy's behavior. I received a panicked phone call from the parents before the staffing to change his placement to behavior disordered. In addition to smearing, their son was beginning to wake up crying with anxiety about going to school and being in trouble. The punishment made no sense to him; it just created more anxiety.

The school and specialists had been treating the symptom (smearing) as if the child was consciously choosing that behavior. I decided to play detective for internal triggers. The first step was to analyze this boy's sensory system — which systems were calming and which were innervating. From previous work with the child, I knew he was extremely olfactory sensitive — he smelled everything! He had done well in school for six weeks, the typical review period. Now, the academics were becoming harder. One characteristic in this boy's profile was a perfectionistic tendency with an obsessive-compulsive piece of the syndrome. His need to get all the answers right was creating a lot of anxiety. He used smell to calm down and keep his brain (reticular formation) aroused. He had probably discovered by accident that after a bowel movement, reading or math had been easier; he was more focused because of the strong, organic smell he experienced.

My suggestion was to get a small prescription jar, place the strongest smelling cheese they could find in it (strong organic smell) and give the jar to the boy. They could allow him to flip the lid anytime he needed. As a result, he stopped his smearing immediately.

Treating the symptom alone had only confused the issue and wasted a lot of time and money. Parents and professionals need to move beyond the symptom to the reason underlying the child's behavior. I'm not saying the behavior should be allowed, but it's important to acknowledge legitimate neurological reasons underlying behaviors and then program around the trigger.

Another example was a young kindergarten child with autism. The boy's behavior always escalated when the class had language group. Language group was on the floor with limited space boundaries and primarily auditory input. This combination made it demanding for the child to stay focused and attentive. Recess was just before the language group, which should have worked well for the boy. Recess provided an opportunity to pump endorphins and run off anxiety to cope with language group.

When observing, I discovered that the boy didn't get to go out for recess. The reason given was that he broke the rules. The adult in charge blew a whistle to signal the children to stop playing and come in. The little boy with autism ran to the swings and began swinging when the whistle blew. Therefore, he was "disobeying the rules, violating authority," and "setting a bad example" — so he was denied recess. No recess meant no anxiety run-off or neurological down time. So when language group started, this child started bouncing off the walls in behavioral outbursts.

The teachers had treated a symptom and escalated their problem. Further research showed that recess was with kindergarten, first, second, and third grades; two sections of each grade. This child was in the youngest group with a disorder characterized by great anxiety when attempting to interact. Unconsciously, the boy knew that he needed to swing, but there was only one swing set with four swings, usually occupied by older, bigger students. When the bell rang, the other children jumped off the swings and presented the little boy with his chance! He jumped on and swung his heart out so he wouldn't get in trouble in language group.

The boy's internal trigger was telling him to calm his neurological system, not to consciously misbehave and violate a rule. If this child's teachers had understood the reason underlying his behavior, it would have solved a lot of problems. Instead, the problems were escalated by teachers not allowing the child to participate in activity he needed. My suggestion was to give the child a routine to request the swing or reserve a swing for his special needs.

Sometimes the big question is, for whom is the behavior a problem? Are we making a problem when there doesn't need to be one? About the same week as the example above, Calvin and Hobbes printed the cartoon on page 97. It summed up the whole incident perfectly!

Calvin and Hobbes   by Bill Watterson

Modification

When a neurological system is overloaded, the person doesn't always make good decisions in choosing behaviors with which to vent anxiety. When a child with autism chooses an unacceptable behavior, such as biting, his behavior must be modified to something else. To just extinguish the biting pushes the child to discover an alternative behavior to meet his sensory needs. His new choice may be worse than his original behavior.

Part of behavior intervention is to explore modifications in behavior to shape them to be less disruptive or inappropriate. One very effective method is to refocus the child or provide a new stimulus. A child may get caught within anxiety and escalate quickly toward a behavioral outburst. If the parent or teacher can introduce a new focus or stimuli that catches the child's attention, the cycle of escalation may be interrupted or broken.

For example, a boy with autism whom I was observing during math kept shouting to get the cat off the table. The teacher was ignoring the behavior and it was escalating. An aide came up and asked the boy if he had a cat at home. The child answered, "Yes." The aide continued, "Does the cat sometimes get on the table? Do Mom or Dad get upset when the cat gets on the table? Where are you now? Is there a cat at school? Is there a cat on the table here at school?" The boy answered each question appropriately. His brain was engaged in processing the questions and got off the perseverative tangent of screaming at the cat on the table. The exchange calmed him down through a new focus, and he was able to move off the cat topic and do his math.

97

A re-stimulation or refocus can take place in any sensory channel. Introducing a new toy to gain a child's attention may allow the teacher to put a disruptive one away. Disruptive stimuli while a child stands in line in the hallway may be blocked out if a teacher puts a Gameboy® in his hands to keep him occupied.

Familiar routines can also calm down behavior rather than escalate it. A routine will help a child with autism cope with transitions calmly. For example, if clean-up is traumatic for a particular child, develop a routine and make sure it is always followed to ease the child's anxiety of putting favorite toys away. Background music might drown out some of the noise, which could be aversive. Certain items could always be assigned to the child with autism to put away. The teacher could blink the lights to warn the children that clean-up will begin in one minute.

Consider the information presented in Chapter 6, Sensory System Differences, as you apply the behavior management principles presented in this chapter. Chart your analysis of a student's sensory channels and systems that trigger anxiety against those that calm and soothe the child. Analyze the student's internal triggers rather than external behaviors.

Combinations of teaching with an awareness of sensory sensitivities can work very effectively in managing behavior. For example, the child who responds well to deep pressure can be accommodated relatively easily in the classroom setting. An adult can sit behind the child and rub his back, massage his shoulders, or squeeze and release the student's forearm repetitively while he keeps working. The student's focus is more productive on academic material if someone feeds his sensory system needs so he can maintain attention on task. If a portion of the child's energy goes toward stimulating his system to stay calm and attentive, it minimizes his focus on learning.

Other deep-pressure activities include rolling up the student in a gym mat and applying pressure, and having the student wear wristbands or headbands, a baseball cap, or a weighted vest. All of these provide a stimulus to help define the child's body in space and provide the sensory stimulation needed to keep the vestibular system innervated to arouse the cortex and remain calm enough to focus.

A summary of the techniques just discussed is listed below.

Behavior Management Techniques
• Refocus; restimulate
• Routines
• Shape alternate replacement behaviors
• Sensory stimulation

Most of the children I work with have a bag of autism toys that are available to them as needed within a classroom. Nature stores and toy stores hold a world of treasures for sensory systems! In Appendix 7A, page 104, I have listed some of the more common behavior problems with autism and suggested possible toys or activities for modifications. Here are a few comments about modification toys and techniques:

- Don't judge success or failure from the first time. When you introduce a toy, it will be new to the child's sensory system. Don't decide about an item's effectiveness immediately.

- Try to let the sensory system be your guide. A child may flap his arms and scream. The teacher may presume that he needs tactile stimulation and not shape his behavior successfully. Perhaps the child needs auditory stimulation rather than tactile, or both. Keep trying to read between the lines!

- I'm always asked how to justify the child with autism's toys to the other students. Tell the children that just as some of them wear glasses to see better, this child needs a Koosh® ball to pay attention better. If the teacher feels too uncomfortable giving the child with autism a Koosh® ball, give out three Koosh® balls; one for the child with autism and two others. The "normal" children will quickly lose interest; the child with autism will need it.

- Be creative. Let the children lead you to their needs. Observe carefully when they are calm or agitated. Capitalize on routines and structure to achieve a comfort zone in the classroom setting. Balance motor movement with quiet time to meet sensory needs.

An example of goals extracted from a case file provides an example of written objectives for behavior. Note the integration of academic, communication/language, and behavior management within the goal progression.

Sample Behavior-Management Goals

I. Jamie's behavior is significantly delayed and similar neurologically to a much younger child. While some characteristics demonstrated are consistent with the internal anxiety and overstimulation within the syndrome of autism, many also appeared to be a manipulative, conscious testing of limits imposed in the school setting. Jamie requires a strict behavior management program to control his physical aggression. As he becomes older, his aggressive hitting, biting, and kicking must be paired with consequences and consistent behavior modification. It is important that he not maintain control in school through disruptive behavior. Offer him choices to create a need for him to communicate. If Jamie has more control over his world, his behavioral disruptions may decrease while his communication increases. The following behavior goals are suggested.

A. Jamie needs to learn that aggressive behaviors are not acceptable and will not be tolerated. Implement shaping, replacement, and punishment/consequences to address and fade these behaviors. For example, when Jamie hits someone, replace the person with a punching bag and train that "if you must hit, you cannot hit people, only the bag." When he kicks someone, replace

the person with a kickball; that is the only thing he can kick. This method respects his possible need to vent through physically aggressive ways, but not toward people. Use restraint and normal consequences to shape the replacement behaviors.

B. Sensory integration may be more effective and facilitate productive focus if more "flooding" techniques are used to calm Jamie rather than physical exercise. It was reported that the more active sensory stimulation makes Jamie more disruptive and "wired." Use music, deep pressure, watching videos, or listening to stories on cassette tapes to flood his sensory system in a sustained, calming manner.

C. Continue to learn to "read" Jamie's behaviors. Many of his behaviors currently appear to be intentional ways to initiate interaction with adults. Jamie wants personal attention and interaction, but he doesn't know how to request it in a positive way, so he seeks it in a negative manner.

D. Jamie's oral stimulation is becoming problematic in regard to hygiene. School materials should not be allowed in his mouth (e.g., chewing on glue). Remove inappropriate items if he chews on them. Replace his need for oral stimulation with something more appropriate. A mouth guard, bite block, or rubber tube (IV tubing) are options that will prevent damage to his teeth. A cup with water to sip periodically may decrease his licking behavior. Incorporating times for water play may also fill this need.

E. Many problematic behaviors occurred when Jamie had to wait or could not do an activity of his choice. A replacement stimulation at those times may head off the outbursts. For example, when Jamie has to wait, give him something to do or play with such as a tactile self-stimulation toy, a tube to chew on, or Walkman® with music. It may also be appropriate to begin a charting system to develop Jamie's understanding of unacceptable behavior. One option is to use a paper strip with 5 or 10 circles on it and cross them out with a black marker when inappropriate behavior occurs. If one or more circles remain during a designated time period, then Jamie earned down-time activity (water play time or some other motivation, such as a hammock or swing). This system may be able to be coordinated with the picture communication board efforts by showing him choices of pictures for what he is working toward (water play vs. a hammock or a swing). Once he points to one, attach that picture to the sheet where marks go.

F. Jamie's schedule included regular time intervals for physical sensory integration activities. Continue to balance down time and work time to increase productive time in school. Set limits and maintain them consistently. Establish certain routines that Jamie should be able to comply with, such as participation in snack and music. Gradually expand the length of time that he must comply by controlling his impulses and attending to the task. Provide vestibular stimulation (rocking) and tactile stimulation (object in Jamie's hand) during periods in which his compliance and attention is being expanded. These techniques should improve his attending behavior. Increased time in the gym for sensory integration and energy run-off may also be necessary as increased behavioral compliance is expected.

G. Since abstract academic skills are too difficult for Jamie, incorporate functional, concrete activities with obvious cause-effect into his academic work. Examples of appropriate activities might include sorting silverware or colored chips into compartments, matching patterns for stringing beads or arranging items, making snacks such as Kool-Aid® or fruit salad, or watering plants. Jamie needs to learn routines to complete a task that has an established sequence of steps that is always the same. Demonstrate the task with pictures of the sequence and then initiate a routine for independent completion. Jamie needs to see the purpose and have closure through completion rather than putting it away to do again tomorrow.

H. Offer choices whenever possible to increase the power and control apparent within nonverbal communication. *Yes* and *no* are abstract concepts. It may be more appropriate to provide choices of activities rather than asking him, "Do you want to ___?" Make sure choices are extreme at first so that the concept makes sense. For example, have two foods for Jamie to choose, one that he doesn't like and one that he loves; have an activity Jamie likes and one that he usually hates. If he chooses the one he doesn't like, make sure that is what he must do. Make sure the adult also has a choice option in front of Jamie when possible. For example, choose the snack he likes and eat it in front of him. Then, his choice is more likely to be the one he likes since the adult just received it while he watched.

I. Structure academic tasks to include visual-motor techniques to maximize Jamie's ability to understand the task as well as increase his attention toward completion. Be aware of his compulsive tendency toward imposing his own order rather than understanding your directions.

J. Use sabotage effectively to prompt Jamie's intentional, positive interaction. Don't anticipate his needs until it's necessary. Wait a while and let Jamie seek help if a lid is on too tight, the scissors are not in the activity box, etc.

Medications and Vitamins

Professionals and parents frequently ask about the effectiveness of medication in controlling autistic behaviors. Presently, there are no drugs to deal effectively with autism in general.

Autism is a biochemical, neurological disorder. The way the brain reacts to sensory stimuli is different. Adding another artificial chemical (drug or medication) tends to further impact the confusion. The person's neurological system is already struggling to maintain a balance, and gets more thrown off when artificial chemicals are introduced.

Medication is effective in intervening on some specific autism symptoms. For example, medication is required to control seizures. Some sleeping disturbances also respond well to drug intervention. Obsessive-compulsive tendencies can also be treated through drug therapy. Since the general anxiety component tends to escalate in adolescence with the hormonal changes of puberty, medication may be beneficial, beginning in the teen years.

Medical research has indicated that most medications for individuals with autism require a minimal dosage. Their systems are usually already sensitive and it is easy to over-medicate within the syndrome of autism. Prescriptions may need to begin at a low dosage initially.

Dr. Bernard Rimland has been conducting some interesting research on the use of vitamin therapy for individuals with autism. Preliminary results have been very positive. Many individuals with autism are picky eaters and do not eat a well-balanced diet. Introducing megadoses of vitamins seems to balance out some of the chemicals in a positive way. Side effects are minimal since the vitamins are derived from natural substances. A prescription isn't necessary, but medical consultation is important in exploring this option. A chart of preliminary studies is included in Appendix 7B, page 105-106. Notice that the positive effects of vitamins are greater than all the medications with one exception. Side effects are also minimal with vitamins compared to side effects with medications.

Parents and professionals also need to probe any sudden onset of significant behavioral changes. Children with autism are not always accurate communicators. Legitimate health concerns may be missed through the haze of inappropriate behavior. Because pain receptors react differently in autism, communicating about health problems can be a guessing game for parents and professionals. These children are also susceptible to the typical childhood ailments, and can be very confused by itchy spots on their stomachs! The reverse can also be true. Whenever Ryan had a great day with no behavior problems and focused attention, we always suggested that his mom take him to the doctor to check for an ear infection. Almost without fail, when he was getting sick, the school saw good behavior. It was as if his body was busy fighting infection and didn't have time to pump chemicals to interfere with his learning on that particular day.

If a child's behavior is approached logically and from an internal perspective, dramatic progress can be realized. Parents and professionals need to put aside the notion that children with autism are trying to drive them crazy. The child with autism is struggling to make sense of the world and can be very confused and frightened. One example a teacher shared with me to describe a client was "like a deer caught in the headlights." You can often see a panicky look and wild eyes in the child with autism. He wants the professional to help him, not add to his anxiety. Remaining calm and objective when approaching behavior will help immensely!

Summary Comments

➡ Most effective behavior management within autism assumes internal triggers, rather than external triggers. The sensory system sensitivity is a key trigger in biochemical internal responses. Intervention is more effective when parents and professionals approach behavior from an internal chemical balance rather than from external actions. (See Appendix 7B, pages105-106, for specific information.)

➡ Behavior is communication. Learning to read the signs of neurological overload can prevent behavioral escalation within the syndrome of autism. Avoid treating the symptom and look further for the sensory trigger underlying the behavior.

➡ Some behaviors may be legitimate problems which the child with autism cannot communicate. Illness, pain, and allergies are examples of symptoms that can put anyone in a cranky mood. It might be a headache or a toothache that underlies the child's misbehavior.

➡ Autism is a biochemical, neurological disorder. Any symptoms which influence the chemical hormonal balance of a child can affect behavior. The hormones of puberty cause havoc with behavior in all teenagers. Certainly puberty will have an impact in teens with autism.

➡ Beware of quick fixes in the area of behavior. Drugs are not a cure for autism. Medications are only effective for specific symptoms, not for global management of autism. Behavior management programs may work for some children, but not all. A constant, controlled environment may overwhelm some children with autism, resulting in worse behavior rather than better.

➡ Inappropriate behavior can be shaped or modified to less disruptive choices. Respect the need for sensory stimulation or calm-down, but replace disruptive behaviors with more age-appropriate substitutes.

➡ Legitimate, abnormal sensory needs remain a part of life for individuals with autism. Behavior management involves exploring options to satisfy neurological needs. High anxiety triggers behaviors. It is necessary to alleviate anxiety to alleviate behavioral problems.

Appendix 7A: Autism Modification Toys

Behavior Problem	Alternatives	
Mouthing; sucking on materials; teeth grinding	Cup with straw to sip frequently; train a swallow response instead Mouth block (prosthodontist device for TMJ) Mouth guard (protective piece athletes wear; great for older clients) Plastic tubing to chew or suck on (like a medical IV tube) Gak® and other sticky substances	
Hand flapping or finger flicking	Koosh® toy Squish Ball® Beads Slinky®	Silicone gel ball Nerf® ball Hacky Sack®
Yells; makes noises	Walkman® with music Metal hand clickers Music corner — tape recorder, CD, or record player Cheeping chicken (activated via skin contact)	Stories on tape Keys
Visual stimulation; fingers in front of eyes	Kaleidoscope Pinwheel Bubbles	Circling music box Colored oil-and-water drip designs
Shredding	Box of rags to shred	Box of paper to shred
Deep tactile; masturbation	Deep-pressure massage Vibrator on leg, arm Wear a baseball cap Bean bag chair	Brushing Wear a weighted vest Wear a headband or wristband Roll child in blanket/sleeping bag
Vestibular	Swing Rocking chair Merry-go-round	Mini-trampoline Stationary bicycle
Darting	Designated walk path following child's request Relay races with a set route	

Appendix 7B: Data on the Effects of Drugs and Nutrients

ARI FORM 34EE
October 1994

AUTISM RESEARCH INSTITUTE • 4182 Adams Ave., San Diego, CA 92116
PARENT RATINGS OF BEHAVIORAL EFFECTS OF DRUGS AND NUTRIENTS

TREATMENT	NO. OF CASES	% WORSE[A]	% NO EFFECT	% BETTER	BETTER: WORSE
DRUGS					
Nystatin (or Ketoconazole)[B]	208	4	47	49	12.9:1 [D]
Clonidine (Catapres)	118	19	30	51	2.7:1
Naltrexone (Trexan)	111	19	40	41	2.1:1
Beta Blocker (Propranolol, Corgard)	154	17	49	34	2.0:1
Cogentin	47	18	47	35	2.0:1
Deanol (Deaner, DMAE)	169	15	58	27	1.8:1
Phenergan	48	23	37	40	1.7:1
Anafranil (Clompramine)	102	29	24	47	1.6:1
Fenfluramine (Pondimin)	401	20	51	29	1.5:1
Tegretol[C]	673	23	43	34	1.5:1
Lithium	209	24	43	33	1.4:1
Mellaril	1605	27	38	35	1.3:1
Buspar	55	27	38	35	1.3:1
Prolixin	36	33	25	42	1.3:1
Benadryl	1347	22	52	26	1.2:1
Depakene (Valproic Acid)[C]	300	27	42	31	1.1:1
Prozac	206	35	25	40	1.1:1
Atarax/Vistaril (Hydoxyzine)	247	22	54	24	1.1:1
Stelazine	348	28	43	29	1.0:1
Haldol (Haloperidol)	804	38	24	38	1.0:1
Zarontin	64	30	40	30	1.0:1
Tofranil (Imipramine)	325	34	34	32	1.0:1
Dilantin[C]	841	28	47	25	0.9:1
Thorazine (Chlorpromazine)	763	35	40	25	0.7:1
Chloral Hydrate	90	43	27	30	0.7:1
Valium (Diazepam)	550	34	45	21	0.6:1
Ritalin	1661	47	27	26	0.5:1
Cylert (Pemoline)	294	46	32	22	0.5:1
Amphetamine (Dexedrine)	629	50	30	20	0.4:1
Phenobarbital (Luminal)[C]	731	48	35	17	0.4:1
Mysoline[C]	87	53	36	11	0.2:1
NUTRIENTS					
Calcium	97	1	41	58	56.0:1 [D]
Vitamin C	220	3	48	49	18.2:1 [D]
Folic Acid	226	3	53	44	16.5:1 [D]
Vitamin B6 (and magnesium)	2050	5	49	46	9.9:1
Zinc	88	6	44	50	8.8:1 [D]
Dimethylglycine (DMG)	1467	7	52	41	5.9:1
Vitamin B3 (niacin/niacinamide)	49	8	47	45	5.5:1 [D]

A. "Worse" refers to behavior. Drugs, but not nutrients, typically also cause physical problems if used long-term.
B. Nystatin and Ketoconazole are anti-fungal drugs useful only if autism is yeast-related.
C. Figure shows behavioral effects only. Ratings of anticonvulsive effects of these drugs available on request.
D. Better/worse ratios marked "D" are unstable due to small number of cases rated "worse." A small change in "worse" changes the ratio greatly.

Reprinted with permission from the Autism Society of America, 800-3-AUTISM

AUTISM RESEARCH INSTITUTE • 4182 Adams Ave., San Diego, CA 92116

Parent Ratings of the Effectiveness of Drugs and Nutrients

The parents of autistic children represent a vast and important reservoir of information on the benefits—and adverse effects—of the large variety of drugs and other interventions that have been tried with their children. Starting in 1967 the Autism Research Institute has been collecting parent ratings of the usefulness of the many interventions tried on their autistic children.

The data presented in this paper have been collected from the more than 8,700 parents who have filled out our questionnaires designed to collect such information.

In all instances, the parents were asked to rate each of the interventions on a six point scale as follows:

1 = possibly helped a little
3 = some improvement
4 = definitely helped
5 = made a little worse
6 = made much worse

For the purposes of the present table, the parent responses on the six point scale have been combined into three categories: "made worse" (ratings 5 and 6),

"no effect" (ratings 1 and 2), and "made better" (ratings 3 and 4).

For each drug or other treatment the number of cases "made better" was divided by the number "made worse" and the drugs (or other treatments) are listed in order of "helped to harmed" ratios, with the most beneficial treatments at the top of the list and the most harmful at the bottom.

The 31 drugs listed first were prescribed by the child's physician in each case. Note that Ritalin, the drug most often prescribed, is near the bottom of the list. Only 26% of the parents reported improvement while 46% said the child got worse on Ritalin.

The seven substances listed under "Nutrients" do not require a prescription an were in most cases given by parents, on their own, who prefer to use natural substances rather than drugs. Information on the use of vitamin B6 and magnesium in the treatment of autism is available on request form the ARI. As information on the use (dosage, etc.) of the other nutrients becomes available, it will be reported in the *Autism Research Review International*.

DRUGS — ANTICONVULSANT EFFECTS
PARENT RATINGS

TREATMENT	NO. OF CASES	% WORSE	% NO EFFECT	% BETTER	HELPED: WORSENED
Zorontin	11	55		45	N/A
Tegretol	109	9	28	63	7:1
Depakene (Valproic Acid)	66	15	21	64	4:1
Dilantin	85	16	34	49	3:1
Phenobarbital (Luminal)	64	16	36	48	3:1
Mysoline	14	21	36	43	2:1

Reprinted with permission from the Autism Society of America, 800-3-AUTISM

Chapter 8
Classroom Strategies

A teacher was my salvation. . . . didn't see my labels, just the underlying talents. . . . he channeled my fixations into constructive projects. He didn't try to draw me into his world but came instead into my world.

Temple Grandin
Emergence: Labeled Autistic

The brain is made up of many different parts, containing many different abilities. Just because one area is affected doesn't mean others are too. . . . The ability of the brain to compensate for damage by using functions that are still intact is often overlooked.

Donna Williams
Somebody Somewhere

Overview

Professionals working with people with autism are faced with unique individuals who present unique challenges. The perspective with which a professional approaches a child with autism can make a significant difference in the child's academic progress. Autistic symptoms can be viewed as barriers or as challenges to hurdle. Behaviors can be viewed as detriments to placement or as immature communication attempts to help the teacher modify the placement. Disabilities can overshadow abilities or be used to overcome disabilities. Fixations can be punished or be channeled constructively. Is the glass half empty or half full?!

Most professionals tend to function in an efficient routine to meet their job responsibilities. The demands of today's world often necessitate choosing the path of least resistance in planning treatment rather than searching for creative alternatives. Often there are several layers of administration governing decisions and methods. Sometimes experience has shown the professional a "best" way to accomplish goals. At times, it seems overwhelming and unrealistic to do anything more than we are already doing. When attending multidisciplinary staffings, I have often heard, "A child has to be able to ____ to be placed in that classroom."

It is not easy to make special modifications to accommodate individuals. However, there are educational laws which require just that! Professionals have to be willing and able to make reasonable adaptations in rules, schedules, materials, and procedures to accommodate a child with special needs. It is not the responsibility of the child with autism to accommodate a teacher. The student with a disability isn't supposed to be required to accommodate the "normals." I have also heard "if the child lets me know" or "if someone tells me what I have to do." Again, the disabled individual is usually not capable of determining the modifications necessary. Professionals are charged with that responsibility.

There are concrete methods to accommodate a child with autism in the educational setting. This chapter introduces and discusses several options. But there are also attitudinal aspects of intervention that can make a dramatic difference in an individual's ability to learn. The personality and receptiveness of the professional are paramount to any specific methodologies or strategies.

- Accept the child with autism as an individual with specific symptoms, not a label.

- Know the child; interact with the child.

- Explore and baseline functional levels. Don't make presumptions of "can" and "can't do" based on behaviors or appearance alone.

- Encourage and support the child. Be kind and helpful.

- Keep an open mind.

These guidelines may sound simplistic, but they overlay complex issues. For example, many children with autism have one-on-one personal aides. An individual aide often becomes an excuse for the teacher to interact minimally or to attempt little instruction with the child who has autism. The aide, who is not certified or qualified, becomes the child's teacher, suddenly assuming a great deal of responsibility with little support, understanding, or assistance from the professionals.

CHAOS by Brian Shuster

"Oh, good invention, Thag. *Fire*, that's JUST what we needed."

In working with autism, professionals may stumble on a wonderful technique, but find that it requires some fine-tuning, revision, or more time to achieve its true potential. Don't be impatient and throw out techniques without giving them a chance. Don't let criticism or premature judgments of colleagues on the periphery intimidate you. Use your good instincts and sensitive perceptions as your guide in working with these children. The rewards can be wonderfully satisfying!

Reprinted with special permission of King Features Syndicate.

Professionals can make a dramatic difference in the progress made by a student with autism. Remember that the student must be stimulated to learn. If a child is not motivated by the material presented, her progress will be stymied. Her body, senses, and mind must be excited. We all learn better when a topic is interesting to us.

Eye contact is a common goal for children with autism. However, to sit at a desk and prompt, "Look at me. You need to look at me," is not a stimulating way to accomplish eye contact. "Normal" people don't look when there is no reason for eye contact. Something needs to catch your interest and motivate you to look.

Another way to address this idea is that goals cannot be presented in isolation. Instead, present a goal, such as eye contact, in a functional context which promotes eye contact. The person could blow bubbles, eat candy, and give the child a choice for snack, or offer a favorite toy for the child to request.

Motivating a child with autism is a continual challenge. Typical rewards such as stickers or tokens are not particularly effective. As soon as the novelty wears off, its impact tends to fade quickly. Most successful motivational rewards within autism are very functional, concrete items that have an immediate sensory impact on the child. Self-stimulatory toys (e.g., a Koosh® ball, a music box, or pinwheels), edibles (e.g., a sip of juice or cola, candy, or a cracker), and movement activities (e.g., rocking, swinging, or walking) are generally more powerful reinforcements for these children.

Channeling interests and fixations also helps stimulate a child with autism for learning. A child who fixates on model cars may work math problems that use a car in the exercise. For example, instead of just presenting numbers to add, make one number represent a certain number of Mustangs while the second number represents Corvettes. Incorporating the idiosyncratic fixation helps bring a calming stimulus to the academic stress, thereby increasing the student's attention. A specific case example follows to illustrate further.

A high school student with autism was fascinated with model trains. His family had allowed him to take over the family garage, in which he had organized a large, complex, model train display. In his mind, the train display became an amusement park and he was in charge. During peer interactions, the stress of relating usually resulted in launching into stories about his amusement park. This subject calmed him down and was stimulating for him to talk about. Other high school students, however, had little tolerance for his fantasy world.

We were able to introduce the young man to a model train club in the area. The membership was primarily older men in the community who also shared a fascination with model trains. The club was a perfect match! The student, who normally avoided social interaction, was willing to work on social skills in this setting because he wanted to attend the meetings. They were of ultimate interest to him. The stimulation provided enough motivation to work on the skills that normally intimidated him, increasing his anxiety. The older men in the club were very tolerant and pleased that a teenager of the present generation shared their fascination. The young man's fetish was a godsend for them. He was a walking encyclopedia of facts that their fading memories couldn't always recall.

As the young man's social skills improved with the adults in the club, he developed more tolerance to remain calm and interact more appropriately with peers. His discussion of attending club meetings was more believable and was tolerated better by other high school students.

A summary list of stimulation techniques is presented below.

Stimulation Techniques

- Stimulate the senses, mind, and body.

- Incorporate unique interests.

- Motivate with concrete, functional items.

- Use incentives that impact the child.

- Channel fixations in a constructive way.

Multimodality Presentation

The neurological system is different within the disability of autism. Concrete sensory modalities are easier for children with autism to interpret. Many of these children in early education settings are functioning at the sensorimotor stage, the earliest Piagetian stage of development. Concrete, functional experiences make more sense to these children than patterned noise with messages encoded within. Most of the children with autism whom I have observed attached meaning through visual or tactile stimulation in the early intervention years. A teacher might point or do something and the child followed. If the teacher was doing one thing and saying another (e.g., completing a task at the desk while telling the children to line up), the child with autism usually did not comply.

Sometimes professionals talk excessively to students with autism, over-explaining and clarifying. However, the auditory channel is very abstract and meaning is attached through a language code system. Visual and physical stimulation are more concrete and have a functional impact on the child's system. Use visual and tactile presentation whenever possible to accompany spoken messages. Verbal stimulation should be limited and simple so that the child doesn't become overwhelmed by a stimulus that is too abstract to process.

When presenting information to a child with autism, the professional has no way of knowing which sensory channel is turned on and receptive to input. If the child's visual system is aroused, the student may respond to colors the teacher is wearing, movement in the background, or even eye blinks. His auditory channel may not be aroused, and the child may only process verbal information minimally. Therefore, present information in a way that stimulates as many sensory channels as possible.

Use caution when presenting stimuli to ensure accurate sensory processing. Some teachers request eye contact from students when they want verbal attention. For example, a teacher might say, "All eyes up here" or "Everyone needs to be looking at me." What the teacher really wants, though, is for the students to listen. The child with autism may turn on his visual channel and look at the teacher, but not hear a word she says. The child's auditory channel may not be alerted. A verbal child with autism once asked me if it was okay to look at the floor when I talked to her. She was sending a clear message that she needed to choose a neutral visual focus if she needed to pay attention to auditory stimuli. Don't say "look at me" if you mean "listen to me."

There is usually a latency or delay when a child with autism switches sensory channels. The child can't switch sensory modalities quickly until her neurological system has matured. I use the analogy of a VCR; the machine cannot play and record at the same time. Many children with autism will sit in a classroom and not respond. Though professionals may assume that nothing was received during class, a parent may later tell a teacher about a new song that was introduced or various activities that were presented in class. The child with autism was on input mode, and recorded or took in sensory stimuli. At home, the child switched to output and played back the day's events. It takes some time before a student with autism can switch readily from input to output modes, and a latency will be apparent in the meantime.

A summary of ideas for multimodality teaching is presented below.

Multimodality Techniques

- Use visual and tactile stimuli; avoid auditory and verbal stimuli.

- Demonstrate rather than explain something verbally.

- Vary teaching across sensory modalities, one at a time.

- Allow extra time for the child to process between input and output.

Routines

Routines are part of life for all of us. Think about the routine of getting ready in the morning. If a child gets sick, the dog makes a mess, or a long-distance phone call takes fifteen minutes, then you rush out the door wondering if you turned off the coffeepot, if the kids got lunch money, and if you put on your watch! Your normal routine was violated by a change in schedule. The normal "cruise control" of getting ready had to be set aside, resulting in a conscious check of steps in the process.

Why do we have routines? Do you ever arrive at work in the morning and wonder how you got there? If someone asked, you might not even remember passing certain landmarks along the way! Routines allow us to complete mundane tasks on automatic pilot so that we can think about more challenging cognitive tasks, such as a staffing scheduled that morning or techniques to try with a puzzling client.

Routines accomplish the same result in autism, only more dramatically. A consistent routine desensitizes a task and makes it less overwhelming to a child with autism. The routinet gives him a sense of comfort, allowing him to relax. This relaxed state facilitates a more focused effort, and the student's work is a more valid reflection of his ability.

New stimuli can provoke anxiety and be overwhelming to a child with autism. New procedures and sudden changes are intimidating. The child's sensory response can trigger fear and behavioral outbursts. When a routine is in place, the child can control anxiety by locking into the learned routine and completing the steps methodically.

The use of routines can assist a professional significantly in planning intervention for an individual with autism. The concept of rituals should be pervasive throughout the school day to help the child remain calm and productive. Routines can be implemented in numerous ways. Suggestions are summarized below, and explained in the following section.

Implementing Routines

1. Schedule the day.

2. Define physical space.

3. Demonstrate academic tasks.

4. Modify existing routines.

5. Build new routines.

---

1. Schedule the day.

The child with autism needs to know the schedule for a setting. If the setting is a therapy session, post a list of activities to be completed on the board. The activities can be listed by location (e.g., window time, table time, outside time, mirror time, and carpet time), by activity (e.g., music time, making sounds time, and looking at pictures time), or, for older clients, by goal (e.g., review rules for conversation initiation, interpret nonverbal facial expression, role-play small talk, and work on carryover interaction with the office secretary). As each activity is completed, erase it or cross it out.

Classroom teachers should have a schedule in the room or for the child. Many teachers use a Velcro® strip that can be changed from day to day. As an activity is completed, the pictured or written activity can be taken off the board and put back in an envelope.

Children with autism can handle schedule changes if they are given warning. They may not like the change, but they will desensitize over time. Their anxiety can be reduced if they know what to expect. One child I observed sat all through reading perseveratively asking what came after reading. The teacher kept telling the child not to worry about what was after reading. It would have been more effective to tell the child so the unknown became known, alleviating the child's anxiety and allowing her to focus on reading.

2. Define physical space.

Children with autism can have highly sensitive tactile triggers. Infringing on their personal space can be very aversive. In a classroom setting, building a "comfort zone" for the child with autism may be important. A defined physical space can also work to set limits for the child. For example, sitting on the floor can be very anxiety provoking for the child with autism. Other children are squirming and in close proximity. The hypersensitive child could quickly escalate to hitting other children to protect a personal space.

The child who needs sensory stimuli to stay focused, such as rocking or moving, may be disruptive to the other children in the area. Use carpet squares to define a student's physical space on the floor. A child I observed in group time on the floor was sitting on a carpet square slightly behind the other children. I soon discovered why as I watched the boy twist and move around. Yet he never left the carpet square, didn't bother other children unless they invaded his carpet square, and answered every question the teacher asked him appropriately! The same principle can apply to defining an older student's desk or work space. Set the limits to reduce a student's anxiety and build a comfort zone.

3. Demonstrate academic tasks.

The saying that "a picture is worth a thousand words" is very true for the individual with autism. Demonstrating how to do a task is much more effective than explaining the task directions. It is also less threatening to observe an action than to try to relate and process verbal information. In presenting a new task, a good rule of thumb is to always do one practice item.

Matching or pairing builds a connection the child with autism can understand. The child must understand the relationship in a concrete, experiential way before he moves on to abstract relationships.

Children with autism can also have a compulsive need for order. Rather than building with blocks, a child might line the blocks up.

The child is making sense of the stimuli by creating order within his world. It is important to respect that need and understand it before moving the child on to more purposeful use of objects.

> For example, one preschool child spent an enormous amount of time taking apart a puzzle. There was a sensory ordering to the process that was critical to the child's ability to relax and eventually put the puzzle back together. The child would carefully take each piece out, finger it, examine it in the light, smell it, etc., before setting it down and moving on to the next piece. The child put the puzzle back together very quickly and accurately. However, a substitute teacher didn't understand this process and dumped the puzzle pieces on the table for the child to complete. The child erupted in a tantrum because of the betrayal to his need for order.

Many times a professional can use a child's exceptional sense of order to shape appropriate behavior. For example, one assessment tool used to evaluate speech and language development involves matching certain block designs. Examiners often have trouble in explaining to the child to match the given design rather than simply line the blocks up. When you consider the child's need for order, you can conceive of a new strategy to complete that task. Give the child the blocks and let him line them up. Then, match his design, lining up the blocks exactly the way he has. Then, it's your turn. Make a design and see if the child will now match yours. Again, a visual demonstration is much more effective than a verbal explanation.

Spontaneity can threaten the child with autism. To create a comfortable environment for the child to respond, teach in routines. If tasks are always approached in the same way, the child will relax and switch into a routine for certain learning activities. The teacher who provides the same prompts and organization before math each day creates a sense of order to help the child relax and focus; the creative teacher may overwhelm a student with autism through daily innovations.

It is also important that the learning task make sense to the child with autism. A gifted student who could read was struggling to succeed in kindergarten, due to confusion within tasks. For example, a worksheet and teacher direction was to color a school bus purple. The child colored the bus yellow and got it marked wrong. When her mother asked why she had chosen yellow instead of purple, the girl's answer made perfect sense. She told her mother there weren't any purple school buses and the teacher must have been wrong!

A child with autism will resist when a task seems to lack closure or serves no purpose in her mind. Many cause-effect tasks in a school building are excellent, functional activities, such as watering plants, feeding the fish, taking lunch count to the office, and stocking milk or snacks in the cafeteria.

4. Modify existing routines.

Routines within autism become problematic if the person's obsession with sameness results in negative behavior whenever change is introduced. Routines can also exclude people and reinforce interaction with inanimate objects. Rather than fight routines established by the individual with autism, work to modify steps in existing routines to make them more functional. A case example illustrates this concept.

> A preschool boy had learned to climb up a structure, but could not slide down. He also had great difficulty initiating interactions. Consequently, he would sit at the top of the slide until an adult noticed his dilemma and initiated assistance. Often he would become upset while waiting because the perseverative physical routine he enjoyed was interrupted, based on adult availability. So teachers inserted a new step into the routine that involved interaction. The boy went through his normal physical routine, but was told to say "help me" when he arrived at the top. While somewhat intimidating to the boy, this verbal request started interaction that allowed him to resume his pleasurable physical routine. His routine absorbed the new step and got him to initiate meaningful interaction!

Another technique is to alter steps to join a student executing a routine. The following example illustrates this technique.

> A preschool boy had a perseverative routine of putting a puzzle together. The clinician altered the routine by joining the activity and forcing interaction. The clinician kept the puzzle pieces in her area. The child had to say "piece, please" to get the next puzzle piece. The reinforcement of continuing the puzzle was enough to motivate him to interact. The next step was to accomplish turn taking within the routine. The clinician would allow the child to put a piece in the puzzle. Then, she would put a piece in and make him wait. Initially, the child would take the piece out and put it in himself, but gradually he allowed the clinician to take turns.

5. Build new routines.

The student with autism learns more comfortably when a regiment is consistant. Because routines are calming and appealing, they can enhance learning. A case example follows to clarify.

> A family lived almost directly across the street from the elementary school. The goal was for their daughter with autism to walk to school independently. The problem was her lack of environmental awareness for safety procedures in crossing the street. The problem was resolved through the introduction of a new routine. A five-step sequence was established and practiced over and over. The routine incorporated the steps for safely crossing the street (e.g., stop on the curb, look both ways). The routine was practiced verbally through role-play and in real life until the routine developed into a functional reminder that enabled the girl to cross the street safely by herself.

While some people may object to this example, the same principle was taught to me in driver's education for the sequence of checks before you turn on the car (e.g., check the mirrors and fasten the seat belt). A routine allows us to complete tasks automatically. For the individual with autism, routines can make it easier to complete tasks calmly and with control.

Providing Choices

Control in an intervention setting usually rests completely in the hands of the professional. Most children tolerate that lack of control and respond well to imposed limits. For an individual with autism, though, the environment can be intimidating. The added lack of control compounds the child's discomfort, minimizing the child's performance. Providing choices introduces an element of control. It allows the child to predict what stimuli may be presented next. It also helps the professional to facilitate the child's functional interaction.

One very effective, subtle method to introduce interaction is through sabotaging an event in the child's world. By purposely placing an obstacle that interrupts the normal sequence of events, you present the child with a choice of interacting for assistance or forgoing the reinforcing activity. For example, suppose a child with autism enjoys rolling Play-Doh® and usually seeks it independently. The teacher could place the Play-Doh® within sight but out of reach or put the lid on tightly so the child cannot open it independently. The motivation to get the Play-Doh® will provide the incentive to interact by soliciting assistance from an adult. The reward — being able to roll the Play-Doh® — will be immediate.

Children with autism have difficulty understanding the concept of choices. Professionals often make the mistake of providing choices which don't have significant outcomes. A child with autism might be presented with a choice of a snack — a cracker or a cookie. To the child, it may not really make much difference. Consequently, the child doesn't choose and the teacher decides the concept of choices isn't meaningful yet.

Teach the concept of choices in a meaningful way with natural consequences. Choices should be extremes that will make a functional difference for the child. For example, the child can have a snack choice of M&M's® or bran flakes; soda pop or water. The child will probably reach immediately for the desirable item. The same idea can be used in academic activities. The child can go outside to swing or sit at the table for language stimulation questions. Choices should begin as desirable and undesirable extremes, and gradually work toward more equitable selections once the concept is established. Make sure the child experiences the immediate outcome or functional consequence of his choices.

Adding clear structure can also accomplish control in an environment and reduce behavioral manipulation. Many children with autism resist working or fight when they have to leave sensory activities, such as swinging. A battle develops between the professional and child to accomplish productive work. An examination of what promotes manipulative behaviors or avoidance tendencies helps to explain the escalation in undesirable behavior.

A child with autism may be very anxious in school. The professional allows the child to calm down by jumping on a mini-trampoline or riding on a scooter board. When time is up, the child resists. The professional then hesitates to let the child do those activities in the future. From the child's perspective, the sensory activity was calming and enjoyable. But the teacher, not the child, has complete control of when and if the child gets to participate in those activities. The child resists because he doesn't know if he will ever get a chance to do those activities again!

Work time presents the same dilemma for a child with autism. If the child is focused and working well, academic material keeps coming. If the child misbehaves and throws a tantrum, work stops. Thus, the professional reinforces misbehavior to get out of work. Again, the teacher is in control and the child may have no understanding of the parameters that result in work or calming stimulation being placed before him.

Using a timer can work well to structure the day and help the child understand control. To a child, the adult is in control and the only means of gaining control is misbehavior or manipulation. If a timer is in control, negotiation is limited. The child learns a routine that structures work time and play time. Visual timers, such as colored oil and water drip designs, work well to provide an objective control. For example, the child must work until the timer is done. Then, the child can listen to music until the timer is done, then work, and so forth. Control becomes objective once the adult is removed from the process.

Down-time choices (i.e., sensory calming activities) can be presented in conjunction with academic work to increase motivation. For example, before beginning math, give the child a choice of music, a walk, or mini-trampoline time. Place a card with the chosen down-time activity on the child's desk next to the timer while the child works on math. When math time is over, (whether or not the worksheet is completed), the child goes to the down-time activity. The timer provides an objective contract between the professional and child. Manipulation and misbehavior to attain down time are minimized.

The sequence of activities provides another option for choice. You might have a certain number of activities which the child needs to do on a given day. Rather than impose your order throughout the day, give the child control over some of the activities. An example illustrates below.

> A clinician was incorporating the introduction of new foods in order to desensitize a child who was a picky eater. The child knew that each Wednesday was the day to make a snack which he must taste. On some days, his anxiety of facing a new food was overwhelming, preventing him from doing any constructive work until the snack activity was over. On other days, he wanted to work on material and avoid the snack for as long as possible. To relieve his anxiety, the clinician gave the child the choice of sequencing activities to determine when the new food would be introduced.

A summary of ideas for using choices is presented below.

Choice Strategies

- Sabotage to promote interaction

- Extremes vs. mutually-desirable choices

- Visual timers for structure

- Down-time reinforcements

- Sequence of activities

Motor deficits and differences can be exacerbated in a classroom setting. The educational system assumes a certain level of independent motor functioning as academic demands increase. The child who has motor deficits requires programming modifications to compensate for his differences.

Probably the most noticeable and disruptive motor differences within autism are the self-stimulatory movements and behaviors. Teachers can be very confused and frustrated when trying to cope with behaviors such as rocking, spinning, head banging, hysterical laughing, hand flapping, biting, or teeth grinding.

It is important to understand these behaviors as being internal rather than external. Many of the behaviors are a means to control and cope with environmental stimuli. Built-up anxiety and tension must be released, while calming sensations must be generated.

General methods of sensory integration, exercise, and sensory flooding (repetitively and intensely stimulating one sensory modality) are effective in decreasing disruptive behaviors. Modifying inappropriate behaviors through replacement or shaping can also be successful. Simply extinguishing or not allowing a behavior is likely to result in the child generating another behavior that may be more problematic. Instead, choose a replacement behavior and introduce it as a substitute for the undesirable behavior. Specific methods for replacing and shaping were addressed earlier in this chapter and in Chapters 6 and 7.

Motor deficits are frequently part of the autistic syndrome. Compensatory techniques often allow the child to function effectively in the classroom. One major deficit area is fine-motor skills. The ability to program and execute fine-motor movements for writing, cutting, and printing are often impaired. These fine-motor deficits can result in frustration, anxiety, withdrawal or multiple other reactions in the child. The teacher who can compensate and minimize frustration will achieve better cooperation and performance from the student.

The best rule to follow is to evaluate a task and determine its primary focus. If the task's main intent is to develop fine-motor skills, then the child with autism needs to work on developing fine-motor skills with the rest of the class. However, if the task has a cognitive, academic focus, then eliminate the fine-motor demands through compensation. This change allows the child to maintain focus cognitively rather than at a motor-performance level. A few examples may help to clarify.

- A teacher wanted her students to assume responsibility to mark their papers. It was routine that a name must be at the top of papers or the assignment was thrown away. Names were written on the paper first. Then, directions were given and the worksheet was completed. One little girl with autism had obsessive-compulsive tendencies in addition to fine-motor deficits. It took her fifteen minutes to print her name at the top of her paper. She did multiple erasures to accomplish the task exactly the way she wanted. By the time she finally printed her name to her satisfaction, her frustration was high, she had missed the teacher's directions, and her classmates were already finishing the worksheet. Her behavior escalated and her work did not reflect her capabilities. A suggestion to use a stamp with her name or preprinted, self-stick labels resolved the problem. The student was able to assume responsibility for putting her name on her papers, but circumvented the fine-motor deficits that escalated her disruptive behaviors and minimized her academic performance.

- A boy with fine-motor deficits and autism was observed in the classroom completing worksheets. The teacher had generated excellent compensatory techniques to compensate for the child's fine-motor difficulties. For example, a sentence completion worksheet using vocabulary words would have presented problems. The teacher had cut up a second worksheet so the student could glue the vocabulary words in the space rather than write them. Spelling tests were done by dictation to an adult who wrote the letters the child said. He also had the option of taking spelling tests at the computer and typing the words rather than writing them. He used a number strip to complete math problems; an aide would point to the problem, the child would find the answer on the number strip, and the aide would write the number in the appropriate space. The student completed assignments with the rest of class and didn't feel singled out by having to leave or do the tasks later. The teacher usually achieved representative work by allowing the student to stay focused on the academic demand rather than the fine-motor skill.

- A particular state completed one week of standardized achievement tests. A high-functioning child with autism was excluded from the tests after the first year. Exclusion was not unusual for special education students, but the reason was. The child had taken the tests the first year with his class. Multiple-choice questions were answered by filling in an oval with a #2 pencil. This child had fine-motor deficits and perseverative tendencies. The first year, he had perseverated on making perfect dots on the answer sheet. The cognitive achievement test became a fine-motor task in dot making! His poor performance had significantly skewed the district's scores, which upset administrators and parents, so he was excused from the tests. This child was quite capable of performing well on the test if compensation from a fine-motor task to a cognitive task had been provided.

An example of a student's fine-motor difficulties in completing a school worksheet is provided on page 123. The printing suggests that the student is approximately a first or second grader. Most professionals are surprised to learn that the child who completed the form has an IQ of at least 130 and is in sixth grade. However, if we look at this student's cognitive performance rather than her fine-motor, the words reveal some excellent ideas.

The worksheet concerns planning a party. The child's answers, listed below, were the steps to take before, during, and after a party.

Before the party	a. Give out the invitations
	b. Plan the games
	c. Buy the cake
During the party	a. Play the games
	b. Talk
	c. Eat the cake
After the party	a. Clean up
	b. Thank them for coming
	c. Go home

The responses demonstrate good insight for a child with autism, such as the inclusion of talking during the party and thanking guests for coming after the party. Typical autistic tendencies are noted through the need for closure (e.g., go home after the party). The point illustrated is that content may be overlooked due to poor fine-motor performance. Teachers need to discriminate carefully when the essential task is fine-motor and when it is academic. When a cognitive focus is required, don't penalize the student with fine-motor deficits; enable her to compensate.

Organizing the Steps

This worksheet is from *Problem Solving for Teens* by Barbara J. Gray, 1990, LinguiSystems, Inc.

To follow a solution plan, you need to know when to do each step. Think about what to do *before* other activities, *during* the main activity, and *after* the main activity.

Read the problem below. Next, read the solution. Then, list the steps below when you need to do them.

Problem: You need to plan how to celebrate your mother's birthday.

Solution: Give a party for my mother at our house.

Steps:

Before the party:

_____ a. _____

_____ b. _____

_____ c. _____

During the party:

_____ d. _____

_____ e. _____

_____ f. _____

After the party:

_____ g. _____

_____ h. _____

_____ i. _____

What order should you follow in your plan? Write a **1** on the blank in front of the first step, a **2** by what you'd do second, and so on.

123

> The more predictable and calm the voice, the less emotional fear it inspires. Mildly autistic children may emerge as themselves in an environment where they are able to relax, though not enough to "lose themselves."
>
> Donna Williams, *Nobody Nowhere*

Technology has introduced several new options for individuals with autism. Each method provides a more concrete, objective presentation of information. This strategy helps to reduce the stress of relating to people directly. The child with autism may focus better on content when the medium is less overwhelming to his sensitive sensory system.

Video

Most children with autism are captivated by video tapes and certain TV programs. Many parents and teachers report that when all else fails, they turn on the video to calm the child with autism. It is not an aversive medium, but an attractive, calming medium. Therefore, it makes good educational sense to use video and television in a more constructive manner than just for behavioral calming. For example, videos provide an excellent opportunity for presenting educational material to many children with autism.

Dr. Mabel Rice at the University of Kansas has researched the effect of video on language acquisition in children for many years. In a workshop presentation (1988), Dr. Rice summarized some startling statistics on television viewing habits of young children. Viewing time averages two and a half hours per day by age three years and increases to five to six hours per day by school age. Attention was measured by sustained eye contact with the television. A summary of the attention statistics is listed below:

Age	% of attention
1	6%
3-4	67%
5-6	75%

In addition to visual contact, the children are probably listening more frequently than these averages indicate.

Parents may notice that Disney movies hold children's attention, while they grow restless or lose interest in other movies. The creators of

Disney children's movies have done their homework! They use a prescribed format to sustain children's attention, such as a song or music every so many minutes. Talking is limited and interspersed with action, music, and songs.

Research statistics substantiate that TV and video are an appealing medium. Children like to watch and probably listen even more. It is unusual to have to force a child to watch TV! The challenge, then, is not in the medium, but the content and programming presented in the medium.

The research statistics about the negative effects of watching TV and videos are well publicized. The most dramatic effect is a tendency toward violence. Children who watch TV also tend to assume that complex problems can be resolved in a thirty- or sixty-minute time frame. Unrealistic expectations and standards of living can also be problematic as presented on TV.

For parents of a child with autism who has difficulty discriminating fantasy and reality, the typical programs can be a nightmare! A generation of Teenage Mutant Ninja Turtle® fans created chaos for children with autism who couldn't discriminate why it wasn't acceptable to karate kick unsuspecting peers.

The problem is in content of programming, not in the medium. Video as a medium is appealing and children will watch whatever is presented if it is formatted to sustain their interest. If program content is carefully screened, negative effects can be minimized.

For the most part, children with autism are fairly non-critical viewers. The visual images are calming to them and they will watch the screen attentively. Professionals can capitalize on the fascination and calming effects of video in presenting information to these children. While "live" presentation may be threatening, information that is presented through a neutral medium may be assimilated more easily. Children with autism use perseverative repetition to calm themselves. Video can provide the repetition of teaching content that professionals don't have the time to do within a school day. The child's exposure to appropriate models of social interaction, language, and academics is increased significantly through repeated viewing of videos. Material presented at school can be reinforced through a taped video for viewing at home. A summary of positive aspects for using videos with students with autism is listed in the chart on page 126.

Benefits of Video

- Repetition
- Increase models
- Home therapy
- Non-threatening

I'd like to share two examples to illustrate positive effects of video with two clients of different ages.

The first example was a preschool child with autism who was relatively passive in therapy, and sensory-defensive with physical intervention. Speech-language therapy sessions were video-taped for the student clinician's learning process. The child's mother asked if she could get a copy for her husband to view at home. The dubbed copy that was provided produced surprising effects. The mother reported that her child would sit and watch the tape repetitively. The child began echoing and repeating the actions and models after several viewings. Other siblings in the family enjoyed watching their brother on TV, and they began imitating the songs, fingerplays, and language models they viewed on the tape. The father felt more involved, seeing what was presented in therapy. The speech clinician began seeing greater progress from the child between sessions, based on the continuous therapy every day via video at home, rather than live sessions only twice a week.

The second example was from a high school student. A non-verbal girl who communicated via typing was integrated for some classes with regular education students. However, she became overwhelmed quickly by all the stimulation in the classroom and she made verbal, self-stimulatory noises to calm down. The result minimized her ability to participate. The resolution was to video-tape the class. The girl took it home to view in the evening. In a calmer environment, she could listen to the teacher, take notes, and complete assignments to take back the next day. She worked on desensitization and peer interaction during class; her academic learning occurred via video tape at home in the evening.

Computer

The computer provides the same objectivity as a TV for the student with autism. The anxiety of relating to other people is removed, allowing the student to attend more productively. Concepts and academic material can be presented in a medium that the child enjoys. The benefits of computer technology for students with autism are listed below.

```
                        Computers

        • Remove the stress of relating to others

        • Improve reading comprehension

        • Compensate for fine-motor deficits

        • Alternative means of communication
```

Reading with comprehension is often first discovered on a computer among children with autism. It is not unusual to discover a young child with autism who reads the directions on a computer monitor to run a software program successfully.

The computer can provide positive therapeutic effects. Many children resist fine-motor exercises with a professional, but will play Nintendo®, Game Boy®, or other computer simulations which require quick visual and manual dexterity for hours. The perseverance to master certain game programs could be viewed as fine-motor therapy time. Using a computer can also improve attention span. Children can focus for long time periods when the medium is reinforcing and non-threatening. I know one family who made it through long lines at an amusement park with a Game Boy® to occupy their child with autism.

The computer can also provide an alternative means of communication for the higher-functioning, nonverbal individuals with autism. Typing is an excellent compensation for fine-motor skill deficits. Many children with autism use a notebook computer to complete their assignments, take spelling tests and exams, and communicate. New computer technology includes innovations like speech synthesizers to provide auditory models and scanners to minimize required motor movements.

It is important to differentiate computers for play and computers for work. Some children with autism have difficulty discriminating and choose only to entertain themselves on the computer and resist academic material. Clear delineation of tasks needs to be provided.

Whole Language

Children's literature provides a rich source of material for teaching. Within autism, whole-language teaching techniques can serve as a bridge between abstract concepts and functional understanding. Using a children's story to illustrate emotions, problems, and situations provides a functional context for the child. Discussion and follow-up activities help to reinforce the reality of difficult ideas for the child. The actual book supplies repetition and reinforcement of the concepts introduced. A chart summarizing the positive aspects of whole language within autism is presented below.

Whole Language and Autism

- Visual organization

- Repetitive

- Functional

- Reality checks

Illustrations in books help a child with autism to organize language ideas. Sequencing is often accomplished through both visual and language stimulation, as in predictive books such as *Brown Bear, Brown Bear, What Do You See?* Repetitive sentences and story plots provide a model for the child to imitate, as in *The Napping House*. Children's stories apply abstract concepts in a functional way, helping the child with autism make sense of the world. The strategy of constant discussion and questions while reading the story inserts reality checks on the child's understanding of the content. A case example further illustrates benefits of whole-language techniques.

> A high-functioning girl with autism enjoyed the "what if" game. She loved to imagine catastrophic events and "being bad" by constantly asking, "What would happen if I...?" She was content to fantasize for several years, but in fifth or sixth grade, she decided to test consequences in real life. For example, she began hitting other children on the bus rather than asking or imagining what might happen if she did. The book *Alexander and the Terrible, Horrible, No Good, Very Bad Day* was chosen to address the situation. First the book was read, which goes through a boy's day in which everything that can go wrong, does. Then, consequences of various actions in the book were discussed. The follow-up activity was to write a book entitled *Rebekah's Terrible, Horrible, No Good, Very Bad Day*. In the book, the girl could "try on" every "what if" that fascinated her and generate the consequences. Once the book was done, she could read her "what ifs" and think about the consequences in her own book, rather than trying them out in real life. She also enjoyed checking out *Alexander and the Terrible, Horrible, No Good, Very Bad Day* from the library.

Another excellent source of materials for language is the *Amelia Bedelia* series. Children with autism love the main character's title because of the alliteration. Amelia misinterprets directions from her employers on a regular basis by attaching literal meaning to language rather than colloquial interpretations. For example, when told to make a sponge cake, Amelia Bedelia cuts up a sponge and puts it into the cake. Children love the absurdity and can laugh at the pictured situations. The books provide a way to address some of the mistakes children with autism make in missing subtle nuances of social interaction in a non-threatening way.

Summary Comments

> Caring would have been useful had it been channeled into an informed understanding of how to build a world I could have trusted enough to reach out to. Sometimes people must love you enough to declare war. The jump itself through the darkness to the other side was something I had to find the courage and ability to do on my own. As much as one might want to, one cannot save another's spirit. One can only inspire it to fight and save itself. . . .
>
> Donna Williams, *Nobody Nowhere*

This quotation from Donna Williams summarizes professionals' role in attempting intervention with autism. The individual with autism must trust the professional enough to leave the comfort of his internal world. The professional in the external world must somehow communicate to the individual with autism that she understands his needs and will be there to catch him if he falls or becomes frightened. A sensitive caring can be communicated without actual words.

At the same time, the professional can't leave the individual with autism in his internal world. For his own good, the person with autism must face the demons of our external world and conquer them. The professional who intrudes with compassion will still make the child angry. The professional who insists that a child not kick other children but instead kick a ball, may trigger worse behavior from the child. The professional who helps a child modify tactile defensiveness to tolerate being touched may prefer the quiet, passive child in the corner to the screaming child that results during therapy sessions. But that is part of declaring war to help the child function and learn.

The goal is for each individual to attain as much independence as possible. The prognosis improves with early intervention; it does not improve with quiet supervision to maintain a current state of general withdrawal.

The rewards of successfully teaching children with autism are very satisfying. The challenges are unique and push a professional to evaluate old ideas of how to teach children effectively. A few methods and philosophical approaches might have to be replaced with new information and ideas.

Professionals must be able to reach children with autism and draw them out of their internal world. This process can be accomplished by applying some of the intervention strategies presented in this chapter.

➡ Stimulate the mind, body, and senses of the individual with autism.

➡ Teach through multiple sensory channels to enhance learning.

➡ Respect sensory system limitations and latencies in the individual with autism.

➡ Use routines to teach, calm, and control the individual with autism.

➡ Structure the environment in an objective, understandable way.

➡ Allow choices to promote interaction and involvement of the individual with autism.

➡ Explore new technology which minimizes interaction while maximizing the focus for learning.

Chapter 9
Pragmatic Intervention

. . . the meaning carried by intonation and gesture can be completely shut down, leaving the listener with no emotional cues. The meaning behind the significance of social rules can be completely lost, and the comprehension of words can drop away, leaving the listener lost as to both concept and significance.

Donna Williams
Nobody Nowhere

Social Skills

A significant impairment in social interaction is one of the diagnostic criteria for autism. This particular aspect of autism is very pronounced and unusual. Even individuals with Asperger's Syndrome or high-functioning autism have deficits in their awareness of social rules. Impaired social interaction is one piece in the autistic syndrome puzzle that often confounds parents and professionals.

Many aspects of the autistic syndrome can approximate near normal levels of performance, such as intelligence, behavior, and communication. However, without the benefit of direct intervention, the area of pragmatic language skills remains significantly delayed. This area is subtle, and often overlooked by individuals with autism who are already struggling to interpret more concrete stimuli in their environment.

The rules of social interaction permeate our lives constantly in subtle ways. For example, we speak more quietly in a library than on the playground. The individual who doesn't understand these rules can stick out in a crowd as being "weird." While these unwritten rules govern every interaction subtly, they are rarely formally evaluated or targeted in intervention. Most people acquire pragmatic rules through modeling and awareness of other people's interaction styles. People with autism are the exception.

The individual with autism is often overwhelmed by sensory stimuli and tries to cope with anxiety on a regular basis. Interpreting language is a challenge because it is such an abstract symbol system. It takes a sophisticated communicator to interpret the subtle layer of meaning imposed on the actual words spoken. Individuals with autism struggle to ever attain that level of language proficiency.

In addition, colloquial language often uses contradictory words and meanings, such as "great" meaning something bad has happened. The intonation, facial expression, or gesture is a truer representation of meaning than the actual words.

While pragmatic language remains a subtle, abstract variable within interaction, it is valued highly. Cultural expectations include pragmatic language as an important factor in success. Subtle cues within business transactions and polite nuances must be perceived and followed to avoid offending others. The impact of poor pragmatic skills can be very dramatic.

> A young man I worked with was not diagnosed as having autism until the completion of his freshman year of college. He had been accepted at the university solely on his strong academic record, but his ability to function socially on a university campus was poor. His pragmatic immaturity and naïvetè were the characteristics that led to his referral for assessment. The lack of intervention until age twenty had limited his pragmatic development significantly. The young man completed his degree in a highly competitive field. While his academic skills were not a problem, his ability to relate in an office setting compromised his ability to secure employment, even with a college degree.

That is the primary problem with the area of pragmatic language. Everyone expects appropriate social skills to develop, but no one assumes the responsibility to assess and intervene when these skills are weak. Pragmatic language tends to fall through the cracks of professional responsibility, yet it can have a very significant impact on the person's ability to function independently as an adult.

Because pragmatic skills vary by social situation, each team member, professionals and parents, needs to assume some responsibility in fostering their development. Take advantage of natural opportunities that present themselves throughout the day as they occur. Incorporate pragmatic language across every setting on a consistent basis to achieve an impact.

Pragmatic language development includes several aspects of interaction. One major area is discourse or conversational skills, including the ability to initiate conversations, remain on topic, and provide an appropriate amount of information. Another aspect involves nonverbal interaction skills, such as the use of appropriate eye gaze, facial expression, body posture and space, and gestures. The awareness of different speech act functions or purposes is another area, such as asking questions and stating facts or opinions.

The following section includes examples of goals and strategies to develop pragmatic, social rule awareness for individuals with autism.

Goals and Activities

Preschool Children

Preschool programs are ideal for promoting social interaction skills in children with autism. The routine has more of a play base with focused work and group times interspersed. Social skills need to be developed within a group setting, but they require an adult model. Peers are fairly unpredictable and intimidating to the child with autism. Social awareness goals can be targeted with adult interaction first. One or two peers can gradually be introduced into a routine, and eventually, the adult can be faded.

A sample routine for a two-hour preschool social skills group is presented below. Note the variety and balance of activities throughout the morning.

Social Skills Preschool Group Schedule

9:00 - 9:20	Free Play
9:20 - 9:30	Movement-Based Teaching
9:30 - 9:40	Quiet Group Teaching
9:40 - 9:50	Music/Songs
9:50 - 10:00	Restroom and Wash Hands
10:00 - 10:15	Snack
10:15 - 10:25	Group Movement Teaching
10:25 - 10:35	Quiet Group Teaching
10:35 - 10:45	Gross-Motor Time
10:45 - 10:55	Free Play
10:55 - 11:00	Clean Up and Dismiss

Some general comments about the schedule.

- Motor movement is balanced with quiet sitting time.

- Teaching times are balanced with movement and quiet sitting.

- Free play at the beginning and end of the day allows the child to calm down before beginning the day by choosing his own activities, and to calm down before leaving for the day.

- Sensory integration time is consistent throughout the morning.

- Interaction demands can be varied within each slot for balance.

Adult interaction within components can be intense at first, and then gradually faded as the child develops comfort within the routine. The teacher may also want to designate spaces for each slot. For example, the first quiet group teaching slot will be on carpet squares on the floor; the second slot will be in chairs at tables. This way, the actual materials or content can vary, but the child always knows the physical space in which teaching will occur.

Major goal areas to address at the preschool level are the following:

- Readiness skills and language — basic vocabulary and concept knowledge

- Pragmatic social skills

- Fine-motor and gross-motor skills

Below are sample objectives to develop social skills.

Objectives for Social Skills for Preschoolers

I. (Name) will improve nonverbal pragmatic skills to a more age-appropriate level.
   A. To increase eye contact during structured interaction
   B. To engage in nonverbal, reciprocal play
   C. To display nonverbal, interactive turn-taking
   D. To listen and respond nonverbally to classroom directions
   E. To indicate preferences or needs nonverbally
   F. To initiate nonverbal interaction
   G. To participate in music and language activities nonverbally

II. (Name) will improve verbal pragmatic skills to a more age-appropriate level.
   A. To use verbal social greetings and manners (e.g., *hi, bye, please, thank you, yes, no*)
   B. To engage in verbal, reciprocal play
   C. To display verbal, interactive turn-taking
   D. To imitate verbally or generate simple, nonverbal information
   E. To indicate verbally preferences or needs
   F. To initiate verbal interaction
   G. To participate verbally in music and language activities

---

The goals listed on page 134 would be in addition to any specific readiness, language content, or academic goals. The language teaching objectives, such as shape, color, or animal recognition, would be incorporated into the same activities. Effective intervention at the preschool level should not be one goal per activity. Gross- and fine-motor skill development should be woven into the other goals. The effective teacher will plan activities that can address multiple goals simultaneously, as in the information below.

Sample Activities and Goals

Activity	Goals
Puzzles	Expressive language (naming items pictured)
	Receptive language (choosing pieces named)
	Interactive nonverbal turn-taking (take turns putting pieces in)
	Fine-motor manipulation and perception
Snack Time	Receptive language (choose item named)
	Expressive language (label item desired)
	Social manners (*please, thank you, yes, no*)
	Verbal indication of needs/wants
	Nonverbal turn-taking (waiting for snack)
	Gross- and fine-motor skills

Balance sensory-motor activities with content-based teaching activities. Examples of other activities conducive to preschool goals in all three primary areas (language, social, and motor) include the following:

> sand and water tables (tactile tables)
> blowing bubbles
> finger painting
> musical books
> stacking blocks
> motor-based songs (e.g., "London Bridge," or "Pop Goes the Weasel")
> walks (shape walk, color walk, nature walk)
> Play-Doh®
> swimming
> playground activities (swinging, riding tricycles)

The preschool level of programming provides an introduction to formal schooling. Desensitization to other adults, children, sounds, smells, and activities are part of this process. The subtle aspects of social skills will not emerge early in remediation. However, teaching methods should continue to stimulate and model social awareness. Once a comfort level has been established for the more primary aspects of the school setting, the child can begin focusing on the more subtle components of social interaction.

Remember to introduce social skills, both verbal and nonverbal, with an adult first. A comfortable routine needs to be established before the child will attempt interaction with peers. Carefully choose peers who are more predictable and less likely to intimidate the child with autism. A patient, quiet peer is a good early interaction partner. Establish early levels of social awareness before moving into more sophisticated areas of pragmatic interaction.

School-Aged Children

Pragmatic skills progress into conversational strategies as the child with autism becomes older, providing the child is verbal. Teachers and parents become less tolerant of perceived rudeness in public situations due to pragmatic deficits. We have all been embarrassed by the pre-school child who blurts out inappropriate information in public. Tolerance decreases as the child grows larger and "should know better."

While expectations increase with age, the pragmatic skills of children with autism usually remain concrete. The rules for social awareness remain subtle and difficult to perceive and understand throughout life. Effective intervention for pragmatic deficits at the school age must attempt to teach subtleties and social nuances.

Examples of possible goals to address pragmatic language and social skill development for school-aged children are listed on page 137. Most of these objectives are self-explanatory. However, teaching conversation skills concretely requires some work. One technique I've used successfully is to create the concept of a conversation train. Every conversation has a beginning, just as a train has an engine. Every train also has a purpose, its cargo. A conversation also has a purpose, or message, to carry. Trains have a caboose to signal the end of the train so traffic can resume. Conversations have endings to let people know the topic has been completed and it is time to move on.

In therapy, the conversation train analogy can be used to teach the child with autism to initiate, maintain, and terminate a conversation. The first step is discrimination. The clinician says phrases and the child determines if the phrase is an initiator (engine), maintainer (middle car), or terminator (caboose). Phrases can be written out or spoken. For example, "I have to get going" would be a terminator. "Hi. What's going on?" would be an initiator. "Please meet me at 7:00 in front of the library" would be content or a maintainer.

Once the child can discriminate the various aspects of conversation, then the task is to generate phrases for the differing parts. Other activities might include listening to taped conversations and discriminating phrases, or taking field trips to study conversation trains in action.

Once the clinician is ready to implement working on conversational strategies, prompts are already in place. A child who jumps right in can be told she needs an engine or an initiator. A child who goes on and on and won't let the conversation end needs a reminder to terminate. A small hand clicker can be used to signal an error without interrupting the child verbally.

Effective techniques for addressing pragmatic social skills with school-aged students are the following:

Group therapy with peers

Scripting routines

Role-play

Carryover activities through assignments and field trips

Structured environment and situations with gradual movement toward unstructured, spontaneous situations

Adolescents and Adults

The transition in adult social skills moves toward independent living in the community. The individual with autism must represent himself appropriately in various settings. Increased independence results in an increased need for pragmatic finesse. Interacting with the bank, utility companies, telephone, post office, landlord, and others requires a certain level of social skills. Employment opportunities can be enhanced or hindered by social skills.

Normally, peer interactions transition into gender relationships and dating during adolescence, forming lasting bonds and friendships. This phase can be very confusing and frustrating for the individual with autism, regardless of functioning level. Reading emotional signals and "between the lines" during verbal exchanges can confound a simple message into a complex tangle. The character of Data on "Star Trek, Next Generation" is an example of living in an emotional world without knowing how to process subtle messages or respond.

Examples of objectives for adolescents and adults with autism are listed below.

Objectives for Social Skills for Adolescents and Adults

I. (Name) will demonstrate age-appropriate functional pragmatic skills.
   A. To demonstrate appropriate verbal conversation skills to elicit and convey information
   B. To demonstrate appropriate nonverbal conversation skills to enhance and clarify verbal messages
   C. To perceive and comprehend accurately nonverbal and verbal colloquial conversation techniques

II. (Name) will demonstrate functional problem solving for independent living.
   A. To generate appropriate solutions to interact effectively in the event of household emergencies
   B. To generate appropriate solutions to interact effectively in the event of emergencies in an employment setting

III. (Name) will demonstrate age-appropriate daily living skills.
   A. To demonstrate appropriate nonverbal body language during conversations
   B. To maintain appropriate hygiene and physical appearance for social interaction

---

One effective technique with older students with autism is to use video tapes. Segments from soap operas are ideal to tape and then play back with the volume turned down. Ask the student to discriminate positive and negative interactions based only on nonverbal input. This clinical technique can improve perceptions significantly and help to focus an individual on nonverbal cues for social interaction.

Field trips and community integration become critical as students become older. The opportunity to interact within the community in a natural setting is the best laboratory for motivation and interest. Artificial situations don't contain the same stimuli and anxiety levels for the individual with autism. The closer the learning setting approximates reality, the better the chances that the skills will generalize.

Community Integration

Pragmatic language therapy must be functional. To artificially simulate life situations is only a beginning step in the process. The routine and comfort level realized through role-playing situations must be extended into the actual setting.

Finding time to conduct field trips and integrate students into the community requires some creative planning on the part of professionals in collaboration with parents. "Comp time" situations may need approval of administrators and teachers to accomplish goals realistically. Effective therapy may sometimes necessitate weekend or evening work-related activities, but the cost in time and energy usually pays off!

It is important not to jump too soon into real-life situations. However, avoiding a situation until the individual with autism is ready may postpone carryover forever. The following sequence has worked well in my experience for accomplishing community integration:

• Talk through the situation.

• Research the situation.

• Role-play the situation.

• Observe the situation in real life.

• Experience the situation in real life.

This sequence accomplishes several things. First, a routine is established and tried out several times. Second, the person desensitizes to the situation by anticipating possible events through research, role-play, and observation. Third, generalization is accomplished with a supportive person who can help keep anxiety down when experiencing the "real thing" for the first time. The following example might be helpful.

> One client was terrible at the dentist's office with her mother. The clinician decided to try desensitizing her to the environment. She and the child discussed what happens at the dentist's office and why. The child and teacher went to the library and checked out several books which reviewed the tools and procedures in the dentist's office. The clinician and child role-played going to the dentist. The clinician took the child to a dental lab training school to observe dental students learning how to use the tools and ask questions. Finally, the clinician took the child to the dentist to have her teeth cleaned — with success!

For lower-functioning individuals with autism, task analysis is an excellent technique to build competence in community tasks. Task analysis is a process of breaking down a task into a sequence of small steps. Then, the teacher can begin with full physical assistance, progress to partial physical assistance, and gradually fade through verbal prompts and models to having the student do the task independently. Appendix 9A on page 142 offers an example of task analysis for watering plants.

The goal in community integration is to move from an artificial setting and allow the individual with autism to generalize skills to function independently in the real world. While this integration training requires more effort on the part of professionals, tolerance on the part of the community, and patience on the part of the individual with autism, the benefits far outweigh the disadvantages.

Summary Comments

➡ Pragmatic language skill involves the ability to adapt to various social situations, both verbally and nonverbally. For those with autism, the social interaction deficit can be extremely debilitating. For high-functioning individuals, poor social awareness can limit occupational choices significantly, despite their high intellectual capabilities.

➡ For such a major piece in the autism syndrome, it is discouraging that pragmatic language often falls through the cracks for assessment and intervention. It is not easily remediated, due to the abstractness and subtlety of social cues. Intervention goals for teachers, parents, and other professionals often overlook social skills.

➡ Pragmatic skill development requires direct, sequenced, concrete objectives. Social awareness is not an area that develops on its own without focused attention. Intervention objectives need to begin addressing social awareness during preschool years, and gradually increase in complexity and abstractness into adult years.

➡ One of the hardest parts for clinicians conducting pragmatic language therapy is to confront individuals directly for their pragmatic errors; therapy feels "rude." With experience, the professional realizes that this directness facilitates progress. It is important to de-mystify this vague, abstract area of communication.

➡ Despite the challenges, pragmatic therapy can be one of the most enjoyable areas for remediation. Building social awareness requires a realness that is refreshing to our sometimes sterile intervention settings. Community integration and field trips are essential to generalize pragmatic skills successfully.

Appendix 9A: Task Analysis Sample

Student _____

Objective _____

_____

Rating Scale for Independent Performance

1 complete physical assistance   4 specific spoken prompting

2 partial physical assistance   5 general spoken prompting

3 model or gesture   6 independent; no prompting

Task: Watering Plants

Steps to Perform Task	1	2	3	4	5	6	7	8	9	10
1. Get watering can from shelf.										
2. Take watering can to bathroom sink.										
3. Put watering can under faucet.										
4. Turn on cold water.										
5. Fill watering can with cold water.										
6. Watering can is full when 1 finger from top.										
7. Turn off cold water.										
8. Take watering can to plant.										
9. Pour water on plant for count of 3.										
10. Stop pouring when you get to 3.										
11 Repeat steps 2 through 7 if more water is needed.										
12. Go to next plant.										
13. Repeat steps 9 and 10 for all plants.										
14. Take watering can to sink in bathroom.										
15. Dump extra water in sink.										
16. Put watering can back on shelf.										
17.										
18.										
19.										
20.										

Dates Task Performed

Chapter 10
Home Intervention

This child is not going to be somebody. The child is somebody.

Anonymous

Communicating with Parents

Parents and professionals must share the responsibility of meeting the needs of a child with autism. Intervention techniques should be consistent whenever possible across home and educational environments. As simple as that seems, however, parents' and professionals' perspectives on autism can be very different.

For a parent, this is not a student who occupies an established number of minutes or hours per day in the schedule. This is not a project that can be approached objectively when time allows. This is a person, not a label or a disability. This is a precious gift, part of a family unit, that occupies 24 hours of every day.

Although both parents and professionals dream of children meeting current and future goals, insuring a consistent commitment to a child over time is more critical to a parent. Parents, who may be unfamiliar with the bureaucracy of education or medical professionals, need assurance that services to meet their child's needs will be provided. It is also important that parents feel they are part of the team working to help their child with autism.

The first contact with a team is usually to initiate an evaluation process. Sharing results and introducing a disability label is a delicate process for professionals and parents. No one looks forward to confirming bad news, yet the introduction of a label can be a positive step.

Parents usually suspect something awry in the development of their child, or they wouldn't be seeking an evaluation. While they may not want to hear their fears substantiated, a disability label is not a total surprise. Without identification of the problem, intervention cannot begin. Once a label is determined, intervention can be initiated to begin remediating the disability.

Through experience, I have found the easiest way to introduce a label of autism is to begin by discussing observational impressions. Talk about characteristics observed during the evaluation, and seek expansion and contributions from the parents. For example, "I saw Tim flap his hands very rapidly when someone approached where he was sitting. Do you see that at home? Do you see any other behaviors like this?" Parents may agree and add other instances of self-stimulatory behaviors. Your example provides a non-intimidating invitation to share their own observations as valued components of the evaluation. The parents then feel that you do know their child and have accurate, valid impressions.

Once you and the child's parents have discussed behavioral characteristics, you can approach a composite summary and introduce a label. For example, "When we see a behavioral pattern of self-stimulatory movements, relating poorly to people and the environment, difficulty communicating, and delays across development by age three, it all suggests the disability of autism. The diagnostic criteria for autism is . . . ." Then, you can take each of the criteria and use an example from the shared discussion to illustrate the presence of that characteristic in the child.

Reassure the parents that they are not the cause of their child's autism. There is enough guilt about various "what if's" (e.g., What if I had gotten an evaluation earlier, What if I hadn't had that one glass of wine while I was pregnant, or What if the emotional trauma of Grandma's death. . . ?). We professionals need to let parents know that the "refrigerator parent" myth is long gone. Autism is present at birth and is not caused by poor parenting, inadequate stimulation, or trauma.

It is critical to provide the family with appropriate background reading material. Once the label is mentioned, emotion sets in and parents react to the label; they may not process information presented orally. Provide a packet of information to read once parents reach home and are ready to either support or refute the label with data. Make sure the information is current and nonthreatening for parents. Parents who search out their own printed information often find outdated literature that paints a very bleak picture of autism. Most current literature suggests remarkable progress with early intervention and accurate diagnosis.

I also provide parents with information for support services. Local parent support groups and the state and national association literature are good items to include in the printed packet. One of the most beneficial pieces of information to give parents is the name and telephone number of another parent who has a child with autism. As a professional, you occupy a different category for the parent. You represent the institution; you carry an objectivity. This isn't your child; it is a student or client to you. Parents need to react and ask questions with another parent who has been where they are.

Encourage the parents to call and ask questions once they receive the evaluation report or read the printed information. Over the years, I am amazed at the parents who tell me they were told that their child had autism — and that was all. They weren't given any information, any resources, ideas for help, or explanation of what *autism* was or meant. Stripping away the negative misconceptions about autism and introducing the reality takes time. Explain autism sensitively and individually for the parents as it relates to their child.

If only one parent in a two-parent family is present at a conference when the label of autism is introduced, offer to meet with the other parent. It is very difficult to hear and accept a disability label. It may be even more difficult to try to explain the label to a spouse. The first parent is still struggling to accept and understand the label himself or herself; that parent should not have to explain and justify the label to a spouse. Research has substantiated how stressful a disability can be on a marriage. We professionals should consider thoughtful ways to reduce and control tension between the parents whenever possible. Show that you care and will assist, but you also respect their privacy.

Below is a summary of ideas for introducing the label of autism:

- Discuss behavioral observations of the child jointly (parents and professional).

- Summarize the characteristics as adding up to autism.

- Introduce the label of autism, define it, and apply it by illustrating with specific characteristics of the child.

- Alleviate any guilt regarding cause.

- Provide a packet of selected reading materials for parents to read at home.

- Provide support and resource information, such as other parent contacts and agencies.

- Encourage or schedule follow-up contact to address questions.

- Be sensitive and supportive, but not patronizing.

Once the label of autism has been introduced, make sure the parents remain valued, integral members of the team. Their insights and experiences can very helpful. For example, one very hot summer I decided to take a group of preschool children with autism swimming. Chaos reigned as we went into an echoing locker room with five screaming children to change clothes. However, once in the water, the children became quiet and calm, and began laughing, talking, and interacting! I then remembered what several parents had told me — when all else fails at home, put them in the bathtub for peace.

Parents can benefit from the feedback of professionals. Home is often a comfort world where the children let loose! At school, the children may be more restrained as they try to conform for strangers. Techniques that work at school may give a parent ideas that help in public situations. Stimuli a child may not tolerate with parents, might be desensitized successfully with professionals. For example, the oral cavity is very sensitive and brushing teeth can be a battle for parents at home. The child will often tolerate a routine developed at school with music or sequenced steps in which all the children engage. School might be the first setting chosen to accomplish tooth brushing, with generalization at home to follow later.

Communication channels must be open consistently between home and school settings, especially during the early years. Children with autism are not reliable communicators. Parents struggle to know what went on at school based on limited information from their child. Conversely, teachers lack input from the home setting. Yet consistency and routines are among the best strategies to generalize progress with children who have autism. Many teachers and parents keep a notebook in a child's backpack which can be written on periodically to share information. This strategy provides both home and school settings with a good way to communicate.

Appendix 10A, page156, is an example of a schedule chart for home-school communication. The entire chart does not have to be completed each day, but highlights can be included so that parents can ask specific questions to elicit more accurate information from their children. For example, a parent may ask what the child had for snack at school. The child's answer of "cookie" may not be accurate, but the parent has no way to check. If a teacher wrote in details, the parent could ask more specific questions. For example, "It was someone's birthday today at school. Whose birthday was it? Did she bring a special snack? What did she bring?" This way, the interaction between parent and child becomes more focused and meaningful.

Teachers also realize the benefits of specific home-school communication. At sharing time, student A tells about going to Pizza Hut® for dinner. When child B, with autism, tells about going to Pizza Hut® for dinner, the teacher doesn't know if the child is echoing the first child or telling the truth. A note from home would allow the teacher to ask specific questions, such as "Someone special came to visit you this weekend. Who was it? Where did you go to eat?"

Communication helps form a solid working relationship among parents and professionals. It sends the message that your input is important. Communication back and forth forges a shared bond of responsibility to help a child progress through a disability. It lets the parents know their feedback is important to the professionals and vice versa. A team effort across home and school settings becomes established and maintained. Parents feel like the important team members they really are.

Professionals are sometimes more prepared to function as a team member than a parent. Help parents prepare for staffings by letting them know what to expect, who will be present, and what information they will be asked to share. Make sure the parents' information is not an afterthought, but an integral part of the reporting process among the professionals. Respect and reinforce the parents' efforts; they need extra assurance and confidence to deal with a disability 24 hours of every day.

Parent Roles

Parents play many roles throughout the life of their child with autism. Some roles might require responsibilities that some of these parents are not prepared adequately to assume. Some parents are more comfortable or skilled than others in various aspects of meeting a disabled child's needs. Parents can become lost, overwhelmed, or overzealous in trying to cope. Most parents I encounter are wonderful allies in understanding and dealing with the puzzle of autism, but they are often confused by the many roles they must play.

Marjorie Hanft-Martone, mother to a high-functioning daughter with autism, described the variety of hats she had to wear over the years. In a presentation, she discussed how difficult it was to juggle the various responsibilities and figure out which hat she was supposed to wear in different situations. The six major roles Marjorie identified are listed below, followed by discussion of each role.

Major Parent Roles

1. Case Manager
2. Advocate
3. Diplomat
4. Clinician
5. Politician
6. Mom or Dad

1. Case Manager

Parents are the constant across a child's life. Teachers, schools, specialists, and administrators change, but the parents stay the same. Once a teacher has learned how to work with a child with autism, the year may be over. Each new year is a scary prospect for parents. The risk of starting all over loses time and progress as each professional adjusts to their unique child with autism.

Professionals sometimes make suggestions from year to year that parents have heard before. The parents may feel an idea has been tried over and over without success. Or a new school may want to discontinue a service that parents have seen faded before with detrimental effects. While the parents keep a historical perspective from year to year, they are not employees of the intervention facility. They may carry the least weight in programming decisions at a staffing, even though they know their child better than everyone present. It becomes their responsibility to explain their child's needs, justify requests, and persuade the rest of the team why certain services are necessary. These parents often carry the stigma of "outsiders" among the professionals while they struggle to maintain a consistent program for their child.

> For example, parents I consulted with were very important in communicating the needs of their young son, who was intelligent but nonverbal. The boy required sensory down time on a regular basis for behavior management. From year to year, his teachers gradually faded his breaks while increasing his academic time. A successful kindergarten and first-grade experience gradually regressed into a negative second-grade and third-grade experience. Behavior problems continued to escalate until the middle of third grade, at which time the boy was removed from regular education and placed in a behavior disordered classroom.

> It took almost two years to restore his behavior and program to the level at which he had been successfully functioning in first grade. He integrated back into a regular fifth-grade class after a year and a half in the behavior disordered classroom. The problem stemmed from a lack of understanding on the part of educational staff about the importance of sensory down time. His parents tried hard to communicate its importance, but were not successful in convincing the school staff.

2. Advocate

A parent can sometimes appear pushy to a school staff. Assertiveness can be perceived as aggressiveness. But each parent has to advocate for his or her own child. Teachers and professionals are sometimes told not to request certain high-cost items, such as classroom aides, occupational therapy, or increased speech-language services. A parent is responsible for making sure his or her child's needs are being met effectively.

The professional staff might have to temper the advocacy, but still respect the intent. A school district is not charged with maximizing a child's program, only meeting the child's needs. The Mercedes-Benz is always available, but we can't all afford to buy it. The compromise might be to evaluate what services the school setting can provide — essential services vs. luxury services.

3. Diplomat

Philosophical differences among team members are not unusual. When professionals disagree, the parent and her child may be caught in the middle. It often falls upon the parent to try to resolve differences among professionals diplomatically for her child's best interests.

The diplomat role can assume larger proportions within the family setting. Settling differences between siblings who may not understand special treatment the child with autism receives is not a pleasant parental task. Explaining to well-meaning relatives that time out or stricter discipline won't make the child with autism normal, requires patience.

Compromises, alternatives, and trial periods of placement are all good strategies introduced by a skilled diplomat. The focus has to remain on the child with autism, not individual egos or pride.

4. Teacher/Clinician

What the professional doesn't have time to finish in therapy or in school, often goes home for parents. Material the child with autism won't focus on at school, Mom or Dad or Grandma is supposed to accomplish at home somehow. While generalization of skills across settings is important, the homework assigned to parents must be evaluated carefully.

Home is a comfort world and a place for down time for a child with autism. Some parents become full-time teachers at home, constantly pushing rather than offering unconditional support to their children. The child with autism requires a safe haven. Parents have to play their teacher role with a fine balance.

Sometimes expectations of a home environment aren't realistic. Each child with autism is part of a larger family unit. To expect a parent to capitalize on every opportunity for eliciting a certain instructional target is not realistic. When the phone is ringing, the dog is throwing up, the bus is outside, and the child with autism isn't dressed, it's not a good time to work on zipping skills!

5. Politician

The bureaucracy governing disabilities can be overwhelming to anyone, including a parent. Legal interpretations, financial constraints, allowable services, and so forth, create a jargon jungle. Some administrators operate under a "what the parents don't know, don't tell them" principle. Other administrators want to cover every liability option, and intimidate parents with too much legalese information. The parents finally decide that they must become politically astute to sort out the red tape.

Politics to accomplish services can begin at the neighborhood level, progressing to community, city, county, state, and country levels. Understanding the process is one major hurdle; playing the political games to accomplish a change in procedures is another. A parent's aptitude for politics can range from losing patience and giving up, to lobbying and voicing concerns publicly before the legislature.

Another aspect of the political arena involves attorneys. Many parents of disabled children are vulnerable to legal suggestion, scrupulous or not. Threats of lawsuits are, unfortunately, commonplace; actual litigation is also increasing. It is unfortunate when intervention needs are addressed through a legal proceeding. Emotions run high and nobody is unscathed. A working relationship for future years of interaction with a child can be irreparably harmed. Part of playing politician may be to soothe egos and work out a compromise.

6. Mom or Dad

The role that often comes last, but should be first, is simply parent; to be Mom or Dad, the person who comforts, loves, understands, and supports. The child can become confused among all the roles thrust on parents. It is wonderful to see the big smile when a child with autism recognizes Mom or Dad as the comfort person who is always there for him.

Parents and professionals need to work together to sort out roles, and to decide who functions best in them. Understand the overwhelming task facing a parent of a child with autism and don't expect perfection. Don't ask parents to be supernatural!

A possible source of conflict in parent-professional relationships can arise from the different perspectives they have. Aspects of autism that may concern a parent may not seem as important to the professional, whose focus is different. Primary problems for one group may be secondary to the other. Open communication is the most effective strategy to understand and resolve those differences.

I was once a guest at a lengthy Individual Educational Plan meeting between parents and school professionals. After each professional had shared her goals, the parents were asked for input. The mother said, "This is all fine, but I have two concerns. One, I need help with toileting. Two, I need ideas for getting through the grocery store." The school personnel responded that those were not educational objective areas in which they dealt, so they couldn't help her. She was very frustrated and the meeting escalated into emotional outbursts.

The school failed to listen to the mother's message. They alienated and denigrated her concerns as not worthy. But these two areas had a major impact on her daily life. Even if these areas were not goals to add to the IEP, the professionals could have discussed the issues with her and provided some resources or brainstormed some ideas to assist. The point is, parents' concerns are just as legitimate as school issues and they need to be addressed. Following are three common parent concerns with ideas for assisting.

1. Toileting

Toileting is a major concern for parents of children with autism, especially if a school program won't accept a child until she is toilet trained. Toileting can be challenging for the child with autism due to neurological components of the disability. Her sensory awareness preceding the urge to urinate may not develop until the child is older. Bowel movement can be traumatic sensorially with strong smells and sensations. Some children also fear sloughing off part of themselves.

One good strategy to address toileting is to develop a timed routine. Observe the child's typical patterns for urination or bowel movement and try to time visits to the bathroom to coincide. A regular routine, such as every two hours, is another option.

Desensitizing the child to the process may also be helpful. There are several children's video-tapes available, some of which use an animated cartoon format (e.g., "Once Upon a Potty") or real children singing (e.g., "It's Potty Time") to make the process enjoyable and less intimidating. Using music or a favorite toy during the timed bathroom visit can also be effective. An enjoyable children's book to normalize the process is *Everybody Poops*, also referenced in the back of this book.

2. Transitions

Making changes in the life of a child with autism can be extremely traumatic for everyone involved. One family was moving to a house with a swimming pool specifically for the child with autism, but their son was very upset about leaving the old house and kept crying and reciting their old address.

Transitions from grade to grade, teacher to teacher, and school to school are fairly common and taken for granted by some professionals. However, for parents and children with autism, these transitions are not mundane occurrences. Professionals need to help parents prepare their children for modifications in school, such as using lockers or changing clothes for physical education. Otherwise, a new expectation can trigger behavioral outbursts that are disruptive for all involved. In transitions:

- Desensitize the child to the change.
- Build a comfort zone with the new element.
- Give the child some control in adjusting.
- Prepare the child in small stages when possible.

3. Plateaus and Regression

Professionals don't always understand the extreme reaction of parents when plateaus or regression occurs in a child with autism. One fear of parents that can be lurking behind their questions is that their child with autism has reached his level of potential achievement. When a plateau or regression occurs, the parents are afraid this may finally be the end of progress, or "as good as it gets." Sensitivity to programming scares for parents facilitates a better working relationship.

Plateaus and regression are not unusual in learning. Most normal children experience plateaus prior to acquiring new skills. For example, toddlers experience motor-developmental bursts while speech-language skills plateau. A one-year-old who starts walking slows down in learning new words. Once walking is under control, language development can take neurological precedence again.

In autism, many plateaus or apparent regressions can actually be signs of progress. For example, a child who has used frequent echolalia may not show any phonological or syntactic errors. Suddenly, parents and teachers hear grammatical errors and sound production errors. Panic ensues because the child is losing her speech-language skills! Actually, the child is progressing from using pre-programmed, echoed phrases to trying to generate spontaneous, original phrases. The child's creativity accounts for her errors and is a sign of significant progress.

Another typical example is in the area of behavior. A child with autism may be self-absorbed, quiet, and content in her own world. Following preschool placement, the child may suddenly begin having tantrums and resisting activities. What appears to be behavioral regression may actually be significant progress. Stimuli from the world that was being tuned out before by the child is now eliciting a response. The child has to desensitize to the stimuli, but at least now she is responding and receptive.

It is important for parents and professionals to approach plateaus and regressions objectively. Neurological integration and progress may be occurring and the child with autism needs time to adjust. Don't jump to quick conclusions. Explain to parents that plateaus and regression are part of normal development and not always a detrimental sign.

Shared Experiences

The unique challenges presented by a child with autism are the common bond between parents and professionals on a team. Collaboration among everyone can facilitate an effective working relationship. Parents and professionals can mutually benefit from the experiences. Communication that encourages an open exchange of information maximizes a team's effectiveness. Important experiences to share include:

- Workshop or presentation information

- Access to resource professionals

- Training

- Support Services, such as respite services

- Pertinent published materials

Parents and professionals should not try to intervene in a vacuum. When a person, book, or presentation is helpful, send the reference information to other team members. Make sure that training occurs for teachers each year, as well as parents, aides, and other students. Educate the community so parents have a support system to understand and assist in community settings. Take time to understand the other person's perspective. The goal is the same for everyone on the team — to reach the child within.

Summary Comments

A nice analogy was shared during a parent-professional panel during the 1995 National Conference on Autism, which I've borrowed to summarize this chapter. Imagine a school bus and a child with autism, surrounded by parents and a team of professionals. The typical picture would be all these people working to help the child ride the bus, representing working with the child to make educational progress. However, to intervene on autism effectively, parents and professionals need to let the child drive the bus. The child is in control and determines what he is ready for. Parents and professionals are along for the ride, bumpy or smooth!

The shared role of parents and professionals is to learn to read the signs along the way. An ignored sensory overload "stop" sign can result in a behavioral collision. A clearly marked "one way" road within a routine for learning needs to be respected; going the wrong way will be counter-productive. "Yield" means to wait and not push aggressively into something the child isn't ready for. "Do not enter" communicates a need for down time and space within the child's own world. Warning signs are often present, but ignored by parents and professionals who believe they know better than the driver.

Another insightful visual presentation from the same conference was a mother who had her son's first gym shoe as a baby, and one he was currently wearing as an adolescent. The point made was that a lot of shoes were worn between the two extremes visually represented. Many small steps had to occur to build a bridge of progress from infancy to the present.

Progress and growth don't happen overnight. The steps required for a child with autism may be more extensive, with many small steps in between, when compared to other children. It is not possible to realize the progress within a disability without going through each phase of the process. It requires patience, support, and time.

Here are some tips for parents and professionals working together:

➡ Keep channels of communication open.

➡ Respect each other's opinions and perspectives.

➡ Share information and ideas.

➡ Maintain consistency across settings.

➡ Listen to each other.

➡ Understand differences in each other's roles.

➡ Maintain realistic expectations for each other.

➡ Bolster each other's confidence.

Appendix 10A: Daily Schedule Sample

Student _____   Date _____

8:10 - 8:30 Arrival	8:30 - 8:50 Pledge, Calendar	8:50 - 9:15 Computer, Language	9:15 - 10:00 Reading, Language
10:00 - 10:45 Snack, Play	10:30 - 11:00 TV, Computer	11:00 - 11:30 O.T., Music, Library	11:30 - 12:00 Art, Math
12:00 - 1:30 Lunch, Play, Story	1:30 - 2:00 Spelling, Motor	2:00 - 2:15 Language	2:15 - 2:45 Art, Motor, Language

After-School Activities	Dinner	Evening Activities
Morning Activities	Breakfast	Special Activities & Comments

Please return this chart to school.

Chapter 11
Conclusions

Above all, I would encourage those who have strived to help people like myself that their efforts are not useless. Responding in an indirect or detached manner is not synonymous with indifference.

Donna Williams
Nobody Nowhere

Overview

Autism presents many unique challenges across an individual's lifetime. Within these challenges, there are opportunities to explore programming variables. Innovations, new ideas, research studies, and case studies all continue to expand our horizons of knowledge about autism.

Perhaps the greatest challenge for professionals and parents is to maintain a critical and ethical outlook on autism. Miracle cures, techniques, and programs appear constantly in the literature. We must maintain objectivity when we evaluate programming techniques to ensure accountability in demonstrating progress toward individual needs. We don't have all the answers. Mistakes will be made. Opinions will differ. But the bottom line has to be a unified team effort to help children with autism attain their potential.

An early obstacle is determining the label. The syndrome of autism can be difficult to diagnose and differentiate from other disabilities. Diagnostic criteria rely on careful observation to discriminate key characteristics. Debate regarding responsibility for labeling continues between educational and medical settings.

Autism thrusts a biochemical brick wall into the face of early intervention. Programming has to continually chip away at the biochemical defensiveness to build an appropriate receptive threshold for sensory stimuli. When sensory stimuli start being received through cracks in the wall, the positive progress is balanced with an increased sensory anxiety. The stress of environmental stimuli can be dealt with productively when approached through a neurological perspective. Ideas to program through the stress of anxiety include the following:

- Have clear expectations and rules.
- Be consistent.
- Maintain logical consequences.
- Stay calm.

- Remain objective; don't take behaviors personally.
- Use structure to create a sense of security.
- Create an environment that has comfort zones.
- Allow endorphin activity for double positive effects (cortical arousal and decrease of anxiety).

Placement and programming decisions require a coordinated team effort, founded in mutual respect among professionals and parents. The team responsibilities are shared. Values and philosophies must be explicitly voiced and agreed upon. Adaptations and modifications must be considered to program in the least-restrictive environment. It is not fair to force a child to fit the norm before certain classroom placements become options.

Focused intervention that begins early, significantly improves prognosis. Establishing a reliable communication output system expands vocational opportunities. Yearly staff meetings should continue to refine the educational objectives to find a niche consistent with potential of the student with autism.

Understanding autism with all its neurological connections and ramifications is important in educational programming. Progress in academic development, communication, behavior, and motor skills can be minimized or maximized with an understanding of treatment approach variables. The syndrome of autism can be easily misunderstood, resulting in exacerbating characteristic components. One of the best ways to overcome problems is to educate everyone involved with the individual who has autism.

In-Service Training

> The "dis" in "disability" seemed written in letters ten feet tall; it cast a shadow over the fact there was any ability at all to be found in that word.
>
> Donna Williams, *Somebody Somewhere*

There's a great deal of ability within any disability. My experience suggests that the best offensive strategy is education. I prefer facts to misconceptions and rumors. This book begins in the first chapter by stripping away some of the myths regarding autism. It is a constant demand to reach various populations and continue that process. But I am a strong advocate for in-service training at all levels for peers, parents, and professionals.

Several years ago, a master's thesis by M. Manhart looked at comfort ratings for interacting with four adults viewed during a three-minute video segment. Two were "normal" adults and two were high-functioning with autism. The study was to determine if high-functioning adults with autism were actually perceived differently than "normals." The answer was yes, with an interesting twist which we called the "know" factor. When the raters recognized the individual and knew the person had a disability (autism), the ratings closer approximated normal. In other words, when they knew the reason for the differences, it wasn't perceived as abnormal.

My in-service presentations have several common goals that are accomplished in a variety ways, depending on the audience. The major objectives are outlined below. The goal is to increase understanding in the community immediately surrounding the individual with autism. This supportive network can intervene when the person is confused or overwhelmed. Professionals and parents may not always be present; peers might be.

In-Service Objectives

1. The Concept of "Different"
2. The Concept of "Anxiety"
3. Abilities and Disabilities
4. Goals

---

1. The Concept of "Different"

Preschool: Ask children who have blue eyes to raise their hands; then green eyes, then brown eyes, etc. Then, ask if any of those eyes are bad colors or wrong colors. No, they are just different.

    Ask children who have blond hair to stand up; then black hair, red hair, etc. Then, ask if any of those hair colors are bad or wrong. No, they are just different.

    Ask people who wear glasses to stand up; then people wearing blue jeans, then tennis shoes, etc. Ask if any of those things are wrong or bad. No, they are just different.

    Summarize the concept of *different* by saying that we have differences so we can tell each other apart. The world is a lot more interesting with differences. To be different isn't bad and isn't wrong.

School: Ask the students to write down the name of a color, a shape, a flower, and a bird. Then, ask them all to stand. You are allowed three guesses. If you name their word, they may sit back down. Suppose for colors, you guess green, blue, and red. Then, go around and ask each student standing what his color is. If several have a certain color (e.g., blue), then allow that group to be seated.

After everyone has a turn, ask if anyone standing gave an incorrect answer —- not a color. Did anyone give a bad color? No, these are the different colors, but none is wrong or bad. Repeat for shapes, flowers, and birds in the same way. Summarize that different isn't wrong and isn't bad; it's just different.

Shapes:	circle, square, triangle
Flowers:	rose, daisy, sunflower
Birds:	robin, eagle, blue jay

2. The Concept of "Anxiety"

Preschool: Choose three or four children to be leaders for "Simon Says." Have them stand in front of the room with their backs to the class. Give directions verbally, but get the class to do what you do nonverbally. For example, say "Simon says touch your nose," but then start clapping and get the rest of the class to follow along. Eventually the leaders in front will begin getting anxious and start turning around. At that point, ask what is wrong, focusing on words like *nervous* or *anxious* about doing things differently.

School: Peer pressure usually creates some anxiety about remaining standing on the first exercise. You might also have people sit down before you give them permission. Talk about how it feels to be singled out for being different.

3. Abilities & Disabilities

Preschool: I use the book *Russell Is Extra Special: A Book About Autism for Children* by C. Amenta (1992). I read the story, sometimes skipping or changing some characteristics to match the individual child in the classroom. This is a nice way to point out the strengths and weaknesses that a child might have.

School:	I tell the students they have a classmate with a difference. That difference is a disability called autism. Autism is not something they can catch and I give them a simple definition. Then, I write the word *disability* on the board. I draw a box around the *dis* and another box around *ability*. I point out that the larger part of the word is *ability* and the smaller part is the *dis*. In other words, there is a lot of *ability* in a *disability*.
	Next, I ask the students to tell me some of the abilities the child in their classroom has. As they generate them, I talk about them and list them on the board.
	Finally, I ask the students to tell me some of the disabilities or differences the student has (e.g., things the student might have difficulty with). I list and talk about each difference as students generate the list.

4. Goals

Preschool:	I suggest various things that the preschoolers might be able to do to help the teacher or the student with his or her disability. It might be to keep an eye on the child at recess or sit next to the child at snack.
School:	I distribute a colored index card to each student. Then, we generate one goal for each *dis* listed on the board. For example, if a student plays alone at recess, a goal might be to make sure someone invites her to play. Each student writes the goals on his card. Then, they tape the cards to their desks as a reminder.
College/Adult:	I talk through the disability and its characteristics. I explain the strengths and weaknesses and list ways the audience can assist the person with autism to relax and feel more comfortable. I use concrete examples and role-play when possible.

In all instances, as a result of the in-service, a support network is established to assist the teachers and parents in meeting the needs of the child with autism. In one sixth-grade classroom, a zealous classmate went so far as to write on the calendar who was to sit at lunch with the child who had autism, and a backup in case the main student was absent! Teachers don't have time to carry out generalization to that extreme. Peer students may jump at the chance.

In-service should not be contained to peers. Other teachers and adults in a building need to understand the disability of autism. Pressure from other teachers has been the downfall of many an excellent behavior management program that appeared too permissive to other teachers!

Area parent support groups have also coordinated in-service presentations for the community. Often a pastor, mail carrier, store clerk, or neighbor would like to interact with a child with autism, but isn't sure how to do it or is afraid to set off negative behavior from the child. Educating the immediate community can provide parents with a supportive network around the home environment. The police and medical personnel are also excellent targets for informational in-service meetings.

In-service training should be ongoing. An individual's needs change; progress changes priorities. Parents and professionals can share the responsibility of insuring a comfort level for people who interact with the child with autism.

Factors to Remember

Hope Factor

Disability labels introduce a harsh reality for parents. Once a label is accepted, a grief process begins. Parents tend to feel the wind go out of their sails and they begin re-evaluating all their dreams for a child who has autism. I know that many professionals feel it is their responsibility to "tell it like it is." However, I heard a specialist in the field say that "with autism, one has to remain humble." We still don't know all the answers. How can we tell a parent that this child will never talk as we evaluate the child at age three? I don't think we can. Who are we to predict IQ before any intervention?

I believe you must leave parents with hope. The full realities will be apparent by the time parents need to deal with them. Parents will ask about IQ, speech, and motor skills. I usually say we don't know for sure. We need to see how the child responds over time and specifics can be sorted out in the coming year. Parents will usually see the reality by the time it's necessary.

Trust Factor

A bond of trust can be a tenuous link or a strand of steel. A bridge of trust must be built between the parents and professionals and between the child and the professionals. Usually the parents and child already enjoy that link.

Honesty and sincerity are two of the major beams to form the bridge between parents and professionals. A professional doesn't have to know all the answers, but must admit when he doesn't know and try to find out. A professional doesn't have to be all things for parents. Sometimes the human touch makes the professional more real. Dealing with a child's disability is emotional. Parents need to feel secure enough to show those emotions in a meeting without ramifications or embarrassment. Parents also need to know that the professional really knows their individual child, not statistics on a piece of paper. The child needs to be flesh and blood that moves within the professional's day on a regular basis.

The bond between a professional and child is interesting. Many professionals come on too strong for children with autism. These children need time to create a comfort zone without interference. Their personal space is important, even if they don't respect yours! Most of the children I've interacted with have instinctively read the people with whom they are comfortable. The approach comes from the child, not the teacher. The adult also has to be comfortable with physical interaction. "Hands off" is too austere to comfort or reach a child with autism.

Creativity Factor

The most bizarre things sometimes work with autism! No one could predict it, but someone has to be brave enough to try it. Novelty is noticeable to the child with autism. For example, in a classroom group situation in which all the children are compliant but one, the child with autism will mimic the child who is misbehaving. Why? Because the actions of the group become the backdrop for the novel action that sticks out and gains attention. Thus, the child with autism notices and copies the aberrant behavior.

Professionals like to stay with the traditional techniques; the way it has always been done. Yet the norm probably won't be effective for the child with autism. Consequently, a new idea, something novel, needs to be introduced and tried. It takes confidence to truly be creative. It requires believing in yourself. It also requires being willing to venture into new territory that hasn't been explored before.

It would be nice if there were a book to go look up any scenario within autism and the answer would be provided. However, it isn't going to happen anytime soon! The competent professional has to assimilate the information available, weigh it carefully with knowledge of the syndrome puzzle each child presents, and determine what might work.

Humor Factor

A sense of humor can make a remarkable difference in facing the challenges of autism. It is easy to lose perspective and become totally focused on some small, annoying characteristic. In the bigger picture, that characteristic may not matter after several years.

> I had one mother whose beautiful little girl with autism frequently echoed the "F" word in a loud voice. The mother was too embarrassed to take her daughter anywhere. In this case, Mom's armor was still thickening to fend off the barbs of the world. Some of the situations related were fairly ludicrous. For example, imagine grown men arguing with a small three-year-old to not say the "F"word, while the little girl sweetly echoes everything they say. I'm not suggesting it wasn't traumatic for the mother. I know it was! But after the situation is over, it's important to try to laugh about it, rather than relive the trauma and embarrassment over and over.

Humor can be a great ice-breaker in tense staffings, and an amusing anecdote regarding the child with autism often works wonders. It adds a human touch that helps us all cope with each day's events.

Is a Cat an Autistic Dog?

Strange question? Not really, if you think about it. Dogs are very out-going, accepting, personable creatures. They are easy to train, come when you call them, and unconditionally love you.

On the other hand, cats are independent creatures who keep to themselves, won't respond to their name, are difficult to teach, and choose when they would like attention from you.

The education system is set up for the dogs of the world. The dogs are the norm and easier to deal with. However, we have some cats in the world. They are not lesser animals; they are not bad animals; they are just different animals. Both are still domestic animals in the category of pets.

The challenge for professionals is to program to meet the needs of the cats, aloof, silent, and in their own world. Yet cats are lovable, teachable, and capable of extraordinary things.

Autism. Not wrong; not bad; just different. And wonderfully intriguing!

The poem below was written by David Eastham, a young man with autism. He was nonverbal, but used a typewriter to express himself. His bittersweet poem suggests all the potential present in individuals with autism and it addresses their differences in a positive way. Yet at the end, David felt he had missed the prime time in his life in which a difference could have been made.

Our task is to plant the seeds for future success. We must nurture, water, and plow the seeds until they bloom and become strong, healthy, independent plants. Then, we can truly plow the happiness!

PLOW THE HAPPINESS

LONELY BOY, DO
NOT FEAR
GOD WILL
APPRECIATE WHY
YOU'RE HERE

THE SUN DOES
RISE
THE WIND DOES
BLOW
I LOVE YOU BOY
UNDER THE SKY

PERHAPS YOU'LL
NEVER TALK OR
RUN
BUT YOU'LL SPREAD
JOY AROUND FOR
EVERYONE

USE WHAT GOD HAS
GIVEN YOU
PLOW THE
HAPPINESS
TOO LATE FOR YOU

From *Silent Words* by M. Eastham, 1990. Ottawa, Canada: Oliver Pate.

References

Amenta, Charles A. 1992. *Russell Is Extra Special: A Book About Autism for Children.* New York, N.Y.: Magination Press. (1-800-825-3089)

American Psychiatric Association. 1994. *Diagnostic and Statistical Manual of Mental Disorders, Fourth Edition.* Washington, D.C.: American Psychiatric Association.

Autism: Breaking Through. 1991. Princeton, NJ: Films for the Humanities & Sciences, Inc.

Autism Research Institute. 1994. Parent ratings of the effectiveness of drugs and nutrients. *The Advocate,* 26:(5), 26-27.

Autism Society of America. 1995. 1995 National Conference on Autism Proceedings. Arlington, TX: Future Education, Inc.

Ayres, A. J. 1979. *Sensory Integration and the Child.* Los Angeles, CA: Western Psychological Services.

Biklen, D. 1990. Communication unbound: Autism and praxis. *Harvard Educational Review,* 60 (3), 291-314.

Callahan, M. 1987. *Fighting for Tony.* New York, N.Y.: Simon & Schuster.

Eastham, M. 1990. *Silent Words.* Ottawa, Canada: Oliver Pate.

Gilliam Autism Rating Scale (GARS). 1995. Austin, TX: PRO-ED

Fox, Sherry. 1994. "Educational Strategies Address Pragmatic and Behavioral Deficits in Autism." *ADVANCE for Speech-Language Pathologists & Audiologists,* March 21.

Gaddes, W. H. 1980. *Learning Disabilities and Brain Function.* N.Y., N.Y: Springer-Verlag.

Gelman, J. 1996. "Managing Behavior in Autism." *ADVANCE for Speech-Language Pathologists & Audiologists,* Jan. 8.

Gillingham, G. 1995. *Autism - Handle with Care.* Arlington, TX: Future Education, Inc.

Gomi, T. 1993. *Everyone Poops.* Brooklyn, NY: Kane/Miller Book Publishers.

Grandin, T. 1995. *Thinking in Pictures and other reports from my life with autism.* N.Y, N.Y.: Doubleday.

Grandin, T. & Scariano, M. 1986. *Emergence: Labeled Autistic.* Navato, CA: Arena Press.

Kanner, L. 1943. Autistic disturbances of affective contact. *Nervous Child,* 2:217-250.

Levinson, B. 1988. *Rainman.* United Artists. (Film)

Lowery, C. K., Quinn, K., and Stewart, M. A. 1983. *Serving Autistic Children Within a Large Rural Area: A Resource Manual.* Iowa City, IA: University of Iowa.

Making Contact - Sensory Integration and Autism. 1993. Peoria, IL: Continuing Education Programs of America.

Martin, B. 1983. *Brown Bear, Brown Bear, What Do You See?* N.Y., N.Y.: Henry Holt and Company, Inc.

Parish, P. 1976. *Good Work, Amelia Bedelia.* N.Y., N.Y.: William Morrow and Company, Inc.

Powers, M. D. 1990. *Children with Autism: A Parent's Guide.* MD: Woodbine House.

Quinn, K. and Beisler, J. 1986. *A Curriculum for Educating Autistic Students: A Working Draft.* Volumes I & II. Iowa: Iowa Department of Public Instruction and Grant Wood Area Education Agency.

Rice, M. 1988. "Word Learning of Language Impaired Children When Viewing Television." Illinois Speech-Language-Hearing Association Annual Convention. Chicago, IL.

Tsai, L. Y. 1990. "Definition of Higher Functioning Autism." Annual Conference of the Autism Society of America.

Viorst, J. 1972. *Alexander and the Terrible, Horrible, No Good, Very Bad Day.* N.Y., N.Y: Macmillan Publishing Company.

Wilbarger, P. and Wilbarger, J. 1991. *Sensory Defensiveness in Children: An Intervention Guide for Parents and Other Caregivers.* Hugo, MN: PDP Products.

Williams, D. 1992. *Nobody Nowhere.* N.Y., N.Y.: Random House.

Williams, D. 1994. *Somebody Somewhere.* N.Y., N.Y.: Random House.

Wood, A. 1984. *The Napping House.* N.Y., N.Y: Harcourt Brace Jovanovich Publishers.